easy to make!
Cooking for Friends

Good Housekeeping

easy to make!
Cooking for Friends

COLLINS & BROWN

First published in Great Britain in 2009
by Collins & Brown
10 Southcombe Street
London W14 0RA

An imprint of Anova Books Company Ltd

The Good Housekeeping website is
www.allboutyou.com/goodhousekeeping

1 2 3 4 5 6 7 8 9

ISBN 978-1-84340-551-1

A catalogue record for this book is available from the British
Library.

Reproduction by Dot Gradations UK, Ltd
Printed and bound by Times Offset, Malaysia

This book can be ordered direct from the publisher. Contact the
marketing department, but try your bookshop first.

www.anovabooks.com

NOTES

- Both metric and imperial measures are given for the recipes. Follow either set of measures, not a mixture of both, as they are not interchangeable.
- All spoon measures are level.
  1 tsp = 5ml spoon; 1 tbsp = 15ml spoon.
- Ovens and grills must be preheated to the specified temperature.
- Use sea salt and freshly ground black pepper unless otherwise suggested.
- Fresh herbs should be used unless dried herbs are specified in a recipe.
- Medium eggs should be used except where otherwise specified. Free-range eggs are recommended.
- Note that certain recipes, including mayonnaise, lemon curd and some cold desserts, contain raw or lightly cooked eggs. The young, elderly, pregnant women and anyone with an immune-deficiency disease should avoid these, because of the slight risk of salmonella.
- Calorie, fat and carbohydrate counts per serving are provided for the recipes.

Picture credits
Photographers: Neil Barclay (pages 52, 66, 85); Martin Brigdale (page 102); Nicki Dowey (2, 6, 14, 16, 18, 20, 22, 24, 26, 27, 32, 33, 34, 35, 36, 38, 39, 41, 42, 43, 44, 45, 50, 51, 53, 54, 57, 59, 64, 65, 68, 69, 70, 71, 73, 74, 75, 76, 77, 80, 82, 83, 85, 87, 89, 92, 94, 96, 97, 103, 104, 105, 109, 110, 111, 112, 114, 115, 118, 119, 120, 122, 123, 125); Craig Robertson (25, 48, 55, 58, 60, 61, 86, 88, 90, 93, 99, 106, 117, 126); Lucinda Symons (pages 10, 12, 28).

Contents

Foreword

Cooking for friends is one of life's greatest pleasures. First, there's deciding what to cook, drawing inspiration from gorgeous photographs, reading recipes and imagining the flavours. Then there's the assembling of the ingredients, followed by the creative bit in the kitchen. And finally there's the moment when you add the finishing touches and bring the fruits of your labour to the table – with smiles of appreciation all round. That's the goal, anyway, but it's not always easy to pull off with aplomb!

The key to successful, relaxed entertaining is lots of planning, getting the balance of the menu right, making sure you have everything you need (including crockery, cutlery and serving dishes), knowing how much wine to buy and – most important of all – getting the lion's share of the work done before the doorbell rings. That's where this book comes in.

As well as over 100 triple-tested recipes to inspire you, it's packed with hints and planning tips from the Good Housekeeping experts – whether you're cooking for six or 60. The aim? To make sure the food is delicious and that you enjoy yourself as much as your guests do...

Karen

Karen Barnes
Head of the Good Housekeeping Institute
Good Housekeeping

0

The Basics

Entertaining

Entertaining friends should be fun and relaxing, not only for your guests, but for yourself. Plan ahead and you are much more likely to enjoy the occasion – there's nothing worse than being ill-prepared.

Larger quantities

Bear in mind that if you have doubled or quadrupled recipes they will take longer to cook or reheat than the original recipe. Factor this in to your timeplan on the day.

Planning ahead

Whatever the occasion – an intimate supper for friends, a family Sunday lunch or a celebration buffet for a crowd – planning ahead will ensure your gathering is a success, leaving you calm and stress-free on the day and able to enjoy time with your guests. Once the menu has been decided, make a master shopping list and separate lists of dishes to be prepared ahead, with a note of when to make them. This applies whatever the size of the occasion. Plan fridge and freezer space well ahead of time. For a large party, you may need to put bulky items into cool boxes – make sure you have plenty of cool blocks at the ready in the freezer. Check that you have candles if you plan to use them.

The guests

The type of event you're planning, along with the number of guests and who you're inviting, will be a factor in choosing the menu and how formal or informal it will be – whether a relaxed supper in the kitchen or a formal dinner party.
- Have a budget in mind before you begin and cost out your menus even if it is just a rough estimate.
- Think about the age of your guests. Older people find it awkward to balance plates and glasses to eat and might prefer a sit-down meal.
- Be realistic. If you're a novice cook and like the thought of entertaining, start off with an informal supper for 4-6 people so you don't feel too flustered.
- Find out if any of your guests are vegetarian, or have special dietary requirements, whether religious or medical.

The venue

Before you send out invitations make sure you've thought about all the practicalities.
- Do you have enough space? A sit-down dinner for 50 people may sound wonderful until your guests are packed like sardines around skimpy trestle tables. In that case, would it be better to have a buffet party?
- If you're planning to have lunch outside do you have enough room indoors for all the guests if it rains?
- Is there enough cutlery, plates, serving dishes or glasses? Borrow these from family and friends or, for large parties, check with local supermarkets and off-licences. Many provide a glass hire service and some companies allow you to send them back unwashed for an extra charge.

- Do you have enough chairs – again borrow from friends and family.
- Hire companies can be found on the internet or in the Yellow Pages – you can hire fridges and freezers too.

Do you need extra help?

Don't struggle on your own. Ask friends and family to help out.
- If you're catering for large numbers, enlist help in preparing dishes ahead of time and/or freeze.
- Enlist help on the day in the kitchen. Get family or friends to hand round nibbles and run the bar area, for example.
- If you're friendly with your neighbours, ask to borrow oven and fridge space. Obviously an invitation to the party should be offered too!

Kitchen equipment and preparation

Once you've planned your menu (see page 12), check you have all the correct kitchen equipment and borrow anything you need.
- Is there space in your kitchen to cook, store and reheat the food?
- Do you have enough fridge/freezer space?
- Do you have large enough pans and casseroles?
- If hob/oven space is an issue choose dishes that can be served cold or at room temperature. It is better to serve cold dishes than lukewarm food that may harbour harmful bacteria.
- Bear in mind that dishes will take longer to cook than usual if your oven is crammed with lots of dishes.
- A food processor makes quick work of chopping vegetables or making pastry.

Make a timeplan

Whether it's a small dinner party or a buffet for 100 it's essential to write a timeplan - it saves last-minute panic and will keep you focussed during the day. It doesn't need to be complicated, just a list of tasks next to the time they need to be done and who's doing them. Leave plenty of time to be with your guests too.

Get ahead

This timetable is for a large party (see page 14), but can be used as a checklist, whatever your event.

Up to three months ahead
- Choose your menu and cook recipes that can be frozen
- Make detailed shopping lists, buying all non-perishable items as early as possible
- Don't forget tablecloths, napkins, candles, plenty of rubbish bags, foil, toilet rolls
- Arrange extra help if necessary
- Hire tables, chairs, china and cutlery

A month before
- Order the glasses
- Buy beer, wine, champagne and soft drinks (see page 19 for quantities)
- Order enough ice to chill bottles and to put into drinks
- Order flowers if wished

The week before
- Order fish, poultry and meat from the fishmonger and butcher
- Order vegetables from the greengrocer
- Make sure you have all the cutlery, plates, serving dishes, serving spoons and equipment you need
- Clear enough room in the fridge; hire an extra fridge if necessary

The day before
- Remove ready-prepared dishes from the freezer and defrost at cool room temperature
- Do any last-minute shopping

On the day
- Lay the table before you start cooking – you'll feel calmer and it won't be left until the last minute
- Chill white wine, champagne and beer. Open red wine an hour before serving
- Arrange flowers and table decorations if using and don't let them get in the way of conversation. Keep them pretty but not over-elaborate
- Prepare vegetables and salads a few hours ahead and chill until needed

Before serving
- Warm plates and serving dishes
- Dress salads; add garnishes

Choosing your menu

Now it's time to choose the menu – there are 12 here to get you started, ranging from a no-cook supper and New Year's Eve dinner to an alternative Christmas meal and a wedding feast. Seasonal menus are best as food is cheaper and more readily available.

Ten tips for planning menus

Bear in mind these simple rules and you won't go wrong.

1 It may seem obvious, but always budget the party before you start planning the menu. The more formal the party, the more it is going to cost.

2 Now is not the time to try a new recipe – unless you're a confident cook it will raise your stress levels, and a disaster could snowball and ruin the whole event. If you are determined to try something new, have a small practice run on the family beforehand. As long as you are happy and confident with the dishes you are cooking, they should turn out well.

3 Avoid complicated menus – for example, choose a starter and pudding that can be prepared ahead so that you only have to cope with the main course and vegetables. Even better, choose a menu that can be prepared ahead completely and only needs reheating and garnishing before serving.

4 Choose a balanced menu: for example, pastry shouldn't appear in more than one course; if you're serving a creamy sauce in the starter, avoid cream in the main course. Think about the colours, flavours and textures of the foods – rich and light, sweet and savoury, crunchy and smooth, hot and cold.

5 Serve a heavy main course with simply cooked vegetables.

6 Follow one or two heavy courses with a light pudding, or a light main course with a rich pudding.

7 Keep garnishes and decorations simple and edible – simple presentation is usually more appealing.

8 Select produce in season wherever possible, when it is invariably at its peak for flavour and best value for money.

9 Don't fuss over fresh seasonal ingredients; for example, Jersey Royals are delicious just boiled until tender and then tossed in butter.

10 Don't be tempted to pile up food on the plates – keep it elegant and simple and your guests will feel comfortably full at the end of the meal.

Menu planner

Here are a few menu suggestions for different occasions...

Quick informal supper

- Lemon and Rosemary Olives
- Red Mullet with Cherry Tomatoes and Basil Oil
- Quick Gooey Chocolate Puddings

A special autumn menu

- Parsnip and Pear Soup
- Braised Guinea Fowl and Red Cabbage
- Pear and Ginger Steamed Pudding

An alternative Christmas

- Chicory, Stilton and Walnut Salad
- Fillet of Beef en Croûte
- Chocolate Mousse Roulade

A quick vegetarian menu

- Blinis with Easy Butterbean and Sweet Pepper Hummus
- Mauritian Vegetable Curry
- Nectarines in Spiced Honey and Lemon

A special summer vegetarian menu

- Broad Bean, Pea and Mint Soup
- Sweet Potato and Goat's Cheese Tortilla
- Summer Pudding

Easter Sunday lunch

- Smoked Salmon and Watercress Breadsticks
- Guard of Honour with Hazelnut and Herb Crust
- Rhubarb Crumble Cake

No-cook summer menu

- Mixed Italian Bruschetta
- Chickpea and Chorizo Salad
- Strawberry Brûlée

New Year's Eve dinner

- Smoked Fish Parcels with Dill and Beetroot Dressing
- Venison Wellington
- Champagne Jellies

Buffet for a crowd

- Maple, Ginger and Soy-roasted Gammon
- Leek and Fennel Tart
- Assorted salads
- Marbled Chocolate Cheesecake
- Mango and Lime Mousse

A summer wedding

- Cocktail Rolls
- Feta, Peach and Watercress Salad
- Roasted Salmon
- White Chocolate and Raspberry Tart

A Mediterranean supper

- Squid with Haricot Beans and Rocket
- Simple Paella
- Italian Ice Cream Cake

A French affair

- Moules Marinière
- Coq au Vin
- Glazed Brandied Prune Tart

Cooking for a crowd

Buffets are an ideal way of entertaining a large number of guests, either formally or informally. Holding a fork buffet is an easy way to feed a crowd, while a served, sit-down event is a good way of cutting costs at a wedding breakfast, for example. Whatever the occasion, follow the advice below for an enjoyable, stress-free occasion.

Canapés

Allow 8 to 10 nibbles per person for a drinks party or 4 to 5 if you're serving them before a meal. Start with milder flavours, then build up to spicier nibbles. Finish with sweet canapés to subtly signal that the party is winding down.

How many?

The maximum number you should try to cater for is 100 – anything over that is best left to professionals. The more people you're feeding the less food you'll need to allow per head. For 100 people, 85 portions should be enough. If you're offering a selection of main courses or desserts though, you'll need to over-cater a little as people like to taste a bit of everything. Recruit a few willing helpers for the preparation and the event itself and everything should run smoothly.

Six top tips

1   Decide on the menu well in advance (see page 12). Choose dishes that can be frozen ahead and are easy to portion, such as quiches, pâtés, tarts, pastries, cakes and pies. It will leave you more time on the day to deal with perishable food, such as salads and fresh vegetables.

2   Keep a detailed list of who is doing exactly what.

3   If you're not holding a sit-down buffet, choose food that can be eaten easily with just a fork while standing up.

4   One or two hot dishes such as casseroles or curries are a popular option during colder times of the year.

5   Work out how you can provide tea and coffee for a large number of people – someone may have a tea urn you can borrow.

6   On the day, allow plenty of time to reheat dishes and/or arrange platters of cold food, enlisting help from friends. Make sure you have enough people to pass food around – at least one per 20 guests.

The buffet table

Arranging a buffet table efficiently and attractively is important when catering for large numbers.

- A buffet should look appetising and beautiful but don't be tempted to overcrowd the table with goodies – it's better to offer just a few delicious dishes with well-chosen accompaniments.
- Choose a mouth-watering centrepiece, such as a whole ham or whole poached salmon.
- Arrange the table so that your guests can move easily around it.
- Put the cutlery and plates near to the main dishes.
- Don't put all the food out at once – refill the dishes regularly so that it continues to look attractive.
- Make sure there are enough serving spoons.
- Keep food covered until ready to serve and garnish at the last minute.
- Portion pies and cakes beforehand or get a helper to do it for you – guests can always come back for seconds.
- Regularly clear away rubbish from the table, such as dirty plates and used napkins.

Handy hints

- Save time and energy by using good-quality ingredients, such as mayonnaise livened up with fresh herbs.
- Set aside a separate area for drinks and allocate a helper to run your bar.
- Make ice well in advance, or buy bags of ready-made ice, and store in plastic bags in your freezer. For large parties, fill cool boxes or the bath with ice and water to keep champagne and white wine well chilled.
- If you don't have a dishwasher, decide where to stack dirty plates before the start so that they don't get in the way. Ask someone to look after the washing up. Ensure you have plenty of clean tea towels for drying up.
- Make sure you have plenty of rubbish bags.
- Be ready for spilled food or knocked over glasses of wine. Mop the stain with cold water then top with several layers of kitchen paper. Press firmly to soak up the liquid – do not rub.
- Put candles, glasses and bottles on sturdy tables, well away from the reach of children and pets.
- Warn your neighbours about the party – in case guests park in front of their driveways or there is a lot of noise.

Catering quantities

Approximate quantities to serve 12 people. For 25, multiply the quantities by 2. For 50, multiply by 4. For 75, multiply by 5$\frac{1}{2}$. For 100, multiply by 7.

Starters

Soups 2.6 litres (4$\frac{1}{2}$ pints)
Pâtés 1.1kg (2$\frac{1}{2}$lb)
Smoked salmon 900g (2lb)
Prawns 900g (2lb)

Main dishes

Boneless chicken or turkey 1.8kg (4lb)
Whole chicken allow three 1.4kg (3lb) oven-ready birds
Turkey allow one 5.5kg (12lb) oven-ready bird

Lamb/beef/pork

Boneless 2–2.3kg (4$\frac{1}{2}$–5lb)
On the bone 3.2–3.6kg (7–8lb)
Mince 2kg (4$\frac{1}{2}$lb)

Fish

Whole with head 2.3kg (5lb)
Steaks 12 x 175g (6oz) steaks
Fillets 2kg (4$\frac{1}{2}$lb)
Prawns (main course) 1.4kg (3lb)

Accompaniments

Potatoes:
 Roast and mashed 2kg (4$\frac{1}{2}$lb)
 New 1.8kg (4lb)
Rice and pasta 700g (1$\frac{1}{2}$lb)
Green vegetables 1.4kg (3lb)
Fresh spinach 3.6kg (8lb)

Salads

Tomato 700g (1$\frac{1}{2}$lb)
Salad leaves 2 medium heads
Cucumber 1 large
French dressing 175ml (6fl oz)
Mayonnaise 300ml ($\frac{1}{2}$ pint)

Bread

Fresh uncut bread 1 large loaf
Medium sliced loaf 1 large (approximately 24 slices)

Cheese

For a cheese and wine party 1.4kg (3lb)
To serve at the end of a meal 700g (1$\frac{1}{2}$lb)

Butter

To serve with bread or biscuits and cheese 225g (8oz)
To serve with bread and biscuits and cheese 350g (12oz)
For sandwiches 175g (6oz) softened butter for 12 rounds

Cream

For pudding 600ml (1 pint) single cream
For coffee 300ml ($\frac{1}{2}$ pint)

Coffee and tea

Ground coffee 125g (4oz) for 12 medium cups
Instant 75g (3oz) for 12 large cups
Milk Allow 450ml ($\frac{3}{4}$ pint) for 12 cups of tea

Salads and side dishes

Endlessly versatile and quick and easy to prepare salads can be served as starters, accompaniments or main courses. Many can be prepared ahead, leaving you free to concentrate on other dishes. When entertaining you'll probably want to be a bit more adventurous with side dishes. However, never prepare vegetables hours in advance, leaving them immersed in cold water, as water-soluble vitamins will be lost.

Summer Couscous

To serve 4, you will need:
175g (6oz) baby plum tomatoes, halved, 2 small aubergines, thickly sliced, 2 large yellow peppers, seeded and roughly chopped, 2 red onions, cut into thin wedges, 2 fat garlic cloves, crushed, 5 tbsp olive oil, 250g (9oz) couscous, 400g can chopped tomatoes, 2 tbsp harissa paste, 25g (1oz) toasted pumpkin seeds (optional), 1 large bunch coriander, roughly chopped, salt and ground black pepper.

1 Preheat the oven to 230°C (210°C fan oven) mark 8. Put the vegetables and garlic into a large roasting tin, drizzle over 3 tbsp oil and season with salt and pepper. Toss to coat. Roast for 20 minutes or until tender.

2 Meanwhile, put the couscous into a separate roasting tin and add 300ml (½ pint) cold water. Leave to soak for 5 minutes. Stir in the tomatoes and harissa and drizzle with the remaining oil. Pop in the oven next to the vegetables for 4–5 minutes to warm through.

3 Stir the pumpkin seeds, if you like, and the coriander into the couscous and season. Add the vegetables and stir through.

Beans with Lemon Vinaigrette

To serve 6, you will need:
400g can mixed beans, 400g can chickpeas, 2 shallots, finely chopped, fresh mint sprigs and lemon zest to garnish. **For the vinaigrette:** 2 tbsp lemon juice, 2 tsp clear honey, 8 tbsp extra virgin olive oil, 3 tbsp freshly chopped mint, 4 tbsp freshly chopped flat-leafed parsley, salt and ground black pepper.

1 Drain and rinse the beans and chickpeas, then put into a serving bowl and add the shallots.

2 To make the vinaigrette, whisk together the lemon juice, honey and salt and pepper to taste. Gradually whisk in the oil and stir in the chopped herbs. Just before serving, pour the dressing over the bean mixture and toss well. Transfer the salad to a serving dish, garnish with mint sprigs and lemon zest and serve immediately.

Creamy Potato Salad

To serve 4, you will need:
550g (1¼ lb) new potatoes, 6 tbsp mayonnaise,
2 tbsp crème fraîche, 2 tbsp white wine vinegar,
2 shallots, finely chopped, 4 tbsp chopped gherkins,
2 tbsp olive oil, salt and ground black pepper.

1 Cook the potatoes in a pan of lightly salted boiling water for 15–20 minutes until tender. Drain, leave to cool slightly, then chop.

2 Mix together the mayonnaise, crème fraîche, vinegar, shallots, gherkins and oil. Season with salt and pepper and mix with the potatoes. Leave to cool, then chill until ready to serve.

Classic Coleslaw

To serve 6, you will need:
¼ each medium red and white cabbage, shredded, 1 carrot, grated, 20g (¾ oz) flat-leafed parsley, finely chopped.
For the dressing: 1½ tbsp red wine vinegar, 4 tbsp olive oil, ½ tsp Dijon mustard, salt and ground black pepper.

1 To make the dressing, put the vinegar into a small bowl, add the olive oil and mustard, season well with salt and pepper and mix well.

2 Put the cabbage and carrot into a large bowl and toss to mix well. Add the parsley. Mix the dressing again, pour over the cabbage mixture and toss well to coat.

Orange-glazed Carrots

To serve 8, you will need:
700g (1½ lb) carrots, peeled and cut into thin matchsticks, 50g (2oz) butter, 50g (2oz) light brown sugar, 150ml (¼ pint) orange juice, 150ml (¼ pint) dry white wine, 2 tbsp balsamic vinegar, 2 tbsp freshly chopped flat-leafed parsley, salt and ground black pepper.

1 Put the carrots, butter, sugar, juice, wine and vinegar into a pan, season with salt and pepper and bring to the boil. Reduce the heat and simmer, uncovered, for 10–15 minutes until the carrots are tender and the liquid has evaporated enough to form a glaze.

2 Keep warm, then scatter with parsley just before serving.

Potato Gratin

To serve 8, you will need:
1 clove, 1 small onion, peeled, 600ml (1 pint) milk, 300ml (½ pint) double cream, 1 bay leaf, plus extra to garnish, 1.1kg (2½lb) potatoes, peeled and thickly sliced, 50g (2oz) fresh white breadcrumbs, salt and ground black pepper.

1 Push the clove into the onion. Put into a large pan with the milk, cream and bay leaf. Slowly bring to the boil, then take the pan off the heat and leave to infuse for 30 minutes.

2 Preheat the oven to 180°C (160°C fan oven) mark 4. Discard the clove and bay leaf and finely chop the onion. Put the chopped onion back into the milk and season with salt and pepper. Add the potato slices to the milk and bring to boil, then immediately take the pan off the heat.

3 Using a slotted spoon, transfer the potato slices to a large, shallow ovenproof dish. Pour the milk over and sprinkle with the breadcrumbs. Cook in the oven for about 1¼ hours or until the potatoes are tender and golden brown. Garnish with bay leaves and serve.

Spicy Roasted Roots

To serve 8, you will need:
3 carrots, sliced lengthways, 3 parsnips, sliced lengthways, 3 tbsp olive oil, 1 butternut squash, chopped, 2 red onions, cut into wedges, 2 leeks, sliced, 3 garlic cloves, roughly chopped, 2 tbsp mild curry paste, salt and ground black pepper.

1 Preheat the oven to 200°C (180°C fan oven) mark 6. Put the carrots and parsnips into a large roasting tin, drizzle with 1 tbsp oil and cook for 40 minutes.

2 Add the butternut squash, onions, leeks and garlic to the roasting tin. Season with salt and pepper, then drizzle with the remaining 2 tbsp oil.

3 Roast for 45 minutes until the vegetables are tender and golden. Stir in the curry paste and return to the oven for a further 10 minutes. Serve immediately.

Wine and drinks guide

A celebration wouldn't be the same without some drinks on hand to make the event go with a swing. Wines, sparkling wines and hot or cold punches are ideal party drinks, and easy to serve.

Pre-dinner drinks

An aperitif should stimulate the tastebuds and the appetite. Avoid sweet drinks such as sweet sherry or creamy cocktails. Good choices are fino (dry) sherry, sercial (dry) Madeira, dry vermouths, dry white wines and champagne or dry sparkling wines.

Wine

- Allow one bottle of wine per head, which roughly works out to six glasses each. A litre bottle will provide eight glasses. It's better to have too much than too little. You can buy wine on a sale-or-return basis – check with your local supermarket or off-licence – but to go back, the bottles must be unopened and in a saleable condition. Have both white and red wine available.
- Look at the cost-saving potential of buying wine by the case, or mixed case, as supermarkets and wine merchants usually have special offers on these.
- Choose a wine that's not too high in alcohol – don't go higher than 13% alcohol by volume.
- If you don't have enough glasses, consider hiring them, rather than buying plastic glasses. Most supermarkets and off-licences offer a free service – just make sure you order in good time and return them clean and undamaged. Ask at the store's customer service desk.
- Cool wine quickly in an ice bath – use half ice and half water and put the bottles in to chill for 20 minutes. If you've bought drinks on a sale-or-return basis, remember to put the bottles in a black bin liner before you chill them, securing it tightly so that the bottles stay dry and the labels don't slip off.
- When pouring red or white wine into a glass, only fill the glass one-third to half full at the most. For a red wine, this allows the drinker to swirl it around the glass and aerate it, while, for a white, pouring just a small amount at a time prevents the wine from warming up too quickly in the glass.

Champagne

Champagne is a great way to kick off a party. You can usually save money by buying in bulk.

- Chill champagne for as long as possible. The lower the temperature, the lower the pressure in the bottle, so the cork is less likely to fly off.

- To avoid champagne spilling over as you pour it into flutes, pour a little into a glass first, swirl it, then tip it into the next one. If the glass is wet, less fizz bubbles up.

Non-alcoholic drinks

Make sure you have plenty of soft drinks on hand for those who are driving, pregnant or simply don't drink alcohol (and don't forget the children). Stock up on a range of fruit juices, lemonade, tonic and sparkling water. Try serving a fruit punch made from orange juice, cranberry juice and tonic on ice.

Matching wine with food

Matching the right wine is not as daunting as you may think if you follow this simple guide...

First courses (not soups) salads, cold meats: Any dry to medium white wine but particularly Muscadet, Chablis, Pouilly Fumé.
Soups: Sherry, Madeira, any dry white wine or light dry red wine, but particularly dry Sauternes, Graves.
Fish: Any light dry or medium white wine or a light red, particularly Muscadet, Mosel, Meursault, Chablis, Chardonnay, Hermitage Blanc, Pinot Noir.
Red meat, game: Any sturdy, full-bodied red, particularly Bordeaux, Chianti, Barolo, Côtes du Rhône, Valpolicella, Médoc, St Emilion; New World Cabernet Sauvignon or Shiraz.
White meat (not stuffed or served with creamy sauces): Any full-bodied white or a medium-bodied red, particularly Chianti Classico, Alastian Riesling.
Cheese: Port, or a young red wine such as Beaujolais Nouveau.
Pudding: Any sweet white wine, particularly Asti Spumante, sweet Sauternes, Vouvray, Orange Muscat and Flora, Marsala, sweet Muscatel, champagne.

Serving wine

Wine and champagne are so much more enjoyable to drink if served at the right temperature. Warm white wine and champagne is inexcusable, and chilled red wine (unless young and intended for serving cold) is not at all pleasant.

Many people serve white wine too cold and red wine too warm. The ideal temperature for red is around 15–18°C, with the more tannic wines benefiting from the higher temperature. On a warm day, a brief spell in the fridge will help red wine. For whites, the more powerful wines, like Chardonnay, should be served cool rather than cold, at around 11–15°C, while other whites should be properly cold, at around 6–10°C. The golden rule is it's better too cold than too warm.

Party food will probably take up most, if not all, of your available fridge space. In any case it is a good idea to keep drinks out of the fridge, as frequent opening and shutting of the door will only raise the internal temperature at the expense of the food inside. You will, therefore, need plenty of ice to keep drinks cool.

If you have a lot of wine to chill, use the bath, or a large deep sink if you have one. About an hour before the party, half-fill the bath with ice, pour in some cold water and add the bottles standing them upright and making sure the ice and water come up to their necks. Alternatively, use a clean plastic dustbin or cool boxes as containers. (Some hire companies will loan special plastic bins for cooling wines.)

How much to buy?

Obviously the amount of alcohol you will need depends on how much your guests will drink. For a dinner party, allow 1 or 2 glasses of wine as an aperitif, 1 or 2 glasses with the first course, 2 glasses with the main course and another with the dessert or cheese.

Remember to buy plenty of mineral water – sparkling and still – and fresh fruit juices. For every 10 guests, buy two 1.5 litre bottles of sparkling water and three similar-sized bottles of still water. Don't forget to buy mixers if you are offering spirits.

Wine and Party Drink Checklist

- Champagne and sparkling wine
- Red wine
- White wine
- Beer and lager
- Mineral water, sparkling and natural
- Real fruit juices
- Other soft drinks and squashes for non-drinkers, children, punches and mixers
- Dessert wine or sweet sparkling wine
- Low-alcohol/alcohol-free wines, beer and lager
- Liqueurs, brandies etc., for cocktails
- Mixers
- Fail-safe screwpull corkscrews and wine bottle stoppers – to 're-cork' opened wine bottles
- Plenty of ice and re-usable ice packs.

The cheeseboard

Nowadays, many people prefer to indulge in a plate of cheese and biscuits rather than pudding. At an informal supper for friends you could offer a cheeseboard instead of dessert along with some fresh fruit such as grapes, pears or figs. For more formal occasions, offer the cheeseboard as a separate course, either in the French style before pudding or as an alternative alongside dessert.

- As a rule of thumb, include one hard, one blue and one or two soft cheeses. Alternatively, if you know your guests' tastes well, choose one very good cheese or a plate of unusual goat's cheese, for example.
- Take into account colour, texture and contrast of flavour when choosing cheese.
- The cheese should be at optimum ripeness – if you're lucky enough to have a cheese shop near you the staff should be able to give you advice.
- Store cheese in waxed paper in the fridge, unless you want it to ripen at room temperature.
- Always remove from the fridge and unwrap at least an hour before serving. It will bring out the flavour and prevent the cheese from sweating unattractively when served. Keep lightly covered to prevent drying out.
- Serve on a wooden board, garnished with grapes, figs or sliced pear. Don't overcrowd the board, making sure you leave room for cutting the cheese.
- Serve with crackers or biscuits for cheese, or fresh bread; walnut bread is particularly good. Other good things to serve separately are celery and walnuts.
- Only offer butter if there is hard cheese.
- Leave the rind on when serving cheese – your guests can remove it or eat it as desired. On fresh and mild cheeses and goat's cheese the rind can be eaten; the older the cheese is the less palatable it becomes. On very strong cheeses the rind is inedible.

After dinner

Finishing off a good meal with a well-chosen cheeseboard or perfectly made coffee and liqueurs is an excellent end to an evening.

Liqueur coffees

To make Irish coffee, warm as many heatproof goblets or glasses as needed, then put 25ml (1fl oz) whisky and 1 tsp light brown sugar into each. Pour in piping hot, strong black coffee, leaving a 2.5cm (1in) gap at the top. Slowly pour double cream over the back of a teaspoon into the glass. The cream will float on top of the coffee.
Other liqueur coffees: Rum (Caribbean coffee); kirsch (German coffee); calvados (French coffee); Tia Maria (Calypso coffee). Cointreau and Grand Marnier can also be used if wished.

Petits fours

These small sweet treats are delicious served with coffee at the end of a meal. Make your own if you have time or buy them ready made. Traditional petits fours include little iced cakes, meringues and tiny crumbly biscuits. However, almost any small rich sweets are suitable; chocolate truffles, fudge and mint-flavoured chocolates are popular, as are dates stuffed with almond paste or Turkish delight.

Drinks

The perfect cup of coffee

If you don't have a coffee grinder, buy beans and have them ground at a specialist coffee shop or buy ready-ground from the supermarket. Beans will keep for up to two weeks in the fridge or for 4-5 months in the freezer in an airtight container. Ground coffee will keep for 4-5 weeks in the freezer. Allow 1 dessertspoon per cup or 1 tablespoon per mug. It is better to make it stronger and allow guests to dilute with milk, cream or hot water if they wish.

The following types of coffee are particularly suitable for drinking after dinner:

French roast: a dark coffee, mixed with chicory for a slightly bitter flavour

Italian roast: the strongest blend, often used for espresso

After dinner: a blend of strong-flavoured, dark-roasted beans

To make cafetière coffee:

Boil fresh water. Warm the cafetière with a little of the boiled water. Swirl, then discard. Add the ground coffee. Pour over the just-boiled water (unlike tea, boiling water spoils the flavour). Leave to stand for 4 minutes, then depress the plunger and serve. Drink within 15 minutes to enjoy at its best.

To make filter machine coffee:

Measure the coffee into the filter. Fill the machine with the recommended amount of water, switch on and leave to drip through. Drink the coffee as soon as possible. Leaving it too long to stand on the hot plate will impair the flavour.

After dinner drinks

Now is the time to offer brandy, liqueurs or port with coffee. If you only have the budget to choose one after-dinner drink, then brandy and port are the safe options, especially as the latter can be offered with the cheese course.

Brandy: Serve in balloon-shaped glasses. VSOP (Very Special Old Pale) means that the brandy has matured for at least five years. Cognac and Armagnac mean that the wines from which the brandy was made come from specific regions in France.

Port: Vintage port needs to be decanted, but other ports such as ruby, tawny and white are ready to drink. Ruby port is rich and red, but does not have the subtle maturity of a tawny. White port is made from white grapes and can be served with tonic as a refreshing long drink.

Types of liqueur

Liqueurs should be served in small glasses and the following are a selection of the most popular listed with their predominant flavour:

Amaretto: almond

Benedictine: herby with a brandy base

Calvados: apple brandy

Cassis: blackcurrant (mix with champagne for a Kir Royale)

Cointreau: bitter orange peel

Crème de menthe: mint

Drambuie: whisky and herbs

Grand Marnier: orange-flavoured, based on Cognac

Kahlua: strong Mexican coffee-flavoured

Tia Maria: Blue Mountain coffee, spices and rum

Party cakes

The key to successful cake-making lies in using good-quality ingredients at the right temperature, measuring them accurately – using scales and measuring spoons – and following recipes carefully. Weigh out all the ingredients before you start, using either metric or imperial measures, never a combination of the two. Use the correct size cake tin and line the tin where necessary. Make sure the oven is preheated to the correct temperture.

Rich Fruit Cake

1   Grease and line the cake tin for the size of cake you wish to make (see opposite), using a double thickness of greaseproof paper. Tie a double band of brown paper round the outside.

2   Prepare the ingredients for the appropriate size of cake. Wash and dry all the fruit, if necessary, chopping any over-large pieces, and mix well together in a large bowl. Add the flaked almonds. Sift the flour and spices into another bowl with a pinch of salt.

3   Put the butter, sugar and lemon zest into a bowl and cream together until pale and fluffy. Add the beaten eggs gradually, beating well.

4   Gradually fold the flour lightly into the mixture with a metal spoon, then fold in the brandy. Finally, fold in the fruit and nuts.

5   Turn the mixture into the prepared tin, spreading it evenly and making sure there are no air pockets. Make a hollow in the centre to ensure an even surface when cooked.

6   Stand the tin on newspaper or brown paper in the oven. Bake at 150°C (130°C fan) mark 2 for the time in the chart until a skewer inserted in the centre comes out clean. Cover with greaseproof paper after about 1½ hours.

7   When cooked, leave the cake to cool in the tin before turning out on to a wire rack. Prick the top all over with a fine skewer and slowly pour 2–3 tbsp brandy over it.

8   Wrap the cake in a double thickness of greaseproof paper and place in an airtight tin, or wrap with foil and store in a cool place.

Cook's Tip

If you are making a tiered cake, it is most important for the final overall result to choose the sizes of the tiers carefully, avoiding a combination that would look too heavy. Good proportions for a three-tier cake are 30, 23 and 15cm (12, 9 and 6in).

Quantities and sizes for rich fruit cakes

To make a formal cake for a birthday, wedding or anniversary, the following chart will show you the amount of ingredients required to fill the chosen cake tin or tins, whether round or square.

Note: When baking large cakes, 25cm (10in) and upwards, it is advisable to reduce the oven heat to 130°C (110°C fan) mark 1 after two-thirds of the cooking time

The amounts of almond paste quoted in this chart will give a thin covering. The quantities of Royal Icing should be enough for two coats. If using ready-to-roll fondant icing, use the quantities suggested for Royal Icing as a rough guide.

Size 1

Square tin: 12cm (5in)
Round tin: 15cm (6in)
Time (approx.): 2^1/$_2$–3 hours
Weight when cooked: 1.1kg (2^1/$_2$lb)
225g (8oz) currants, 125g (4oz) each sultanas and raisins, 50g (2oz) glacé cherries, 25g (1oz) each mixed peel and flaked almonds, a little lemon zest, 175g (6oz) plain flour, 4 tsp each mixed spice and cinnamon, 150g (5oz) each softened butter and soft brown sugar, 2^1/$_2$ medium eggs, beaten, 1 tbsp brandy.
Almond paste: 350g (12oz)
Royal icing: 450g (1lb)

Size 2

Square tin: 15cm (6in)
Round tin: 18cm (7in)
Time (approx.): 3 hours
Weight when cooked: 1.6kg (3^1/$_4$lb)
350g (12oz) currants, 125g (4oz) each sultanas and raisins, 75g (3oz) glacé cherries, 50g (2oz) each mixed peel and flaked almonds, a little lemon zest, 200g (7oz) plain flour, ^{1}/$_2$ tsp each mixed spice and cinnamon, 175g (6oz) softened butter and soft brown sugar, 3 medium eggs, beaten, 1 tbsp brandy.
Almond paste: 450g (1lb)
Royal icing: 550g (1^1/$_4$ lb)

Size 3

Square tin: 20cm (8in)
Round tin: 23cm (9in)
Time (approx.): 4 hours
Weight when cooked: 2.7kg (6lb)
625g (1lb 6oz) currants, 225g (8oz) each sultanas and raisins, 175g (6oz) glacé cherries, 125g (4oz) each mixed peel and flaked almonds, zest of ^{1}/$_4$ lemon, 400g (14oz) plain flour, 1 tsp each cinnamon and mixed spice, 350g (12oz) softened butter and soft brown sugar, 6 medium eggs, beaten, 2 tbsp brandy.
Almond paste: 800g (1^3/$_4$lb)
Royal icing: 900g (2lb)

Size 4

Square tin: 23cm (9in)
Round tin: 25cm (10in)
Time (approx.): 6 hours
Weight when cooked: 4kg (9lb)
775g (1lb 12oz) currants, 375g (13oz) each sultanas and raisins, 250g (9oz) glacé cherries, 150g (5oz) each mixed peel and flaked almonds, zest of ^{1}/$_4$ lemon, 600g (1lb 5oz) plain flour, 1 tsp each mixed spice and cinnamon, 500g (1lb 2oz) each softened butter and soft brown sugar, 9 medium eggs, beaten, 2-3 tbsp brandy.
Almond paste: 900g (2lb)
Royal icing: 1kg (2^1/$_4$lb)

Size 5

Square tin: 28cm (11in)
Round tin: 30cm (12in)
Time (approx.): 8 hours
Weight when cooked: 6.7kg (14^3/$_4$lb)
1.5kg (3lb 2oz) currants, 525g (1lb 3oz) each sultanas and raisins, 350g (12oz) glacé cherries, 250g (9oz) each mixed peel and flaked almonds, zest of ^{1}/$_2$ lemon, 825g (1lb 13oz) plain flour, 2^1/$_2$ tsp each mixed spice and cinnamon, 800g (1lb 12oz) each softened butter and soft brown sugar, 14 medium eggs, beaten, 4 tbsp brandy.
Almond paste: 1.1kg (2?lb)
Royal icing: 1.4kg (3lb)

Size 6

Square tin: 30cm (12in)
Round tin: 33cm (13in)
Time (approx.): 8^1/$_2$ hours
Weight when cooked: 7.7kg (17lb)
1.7kg (3lb 12oz) currants, 625g (1lb 6oz) each sultanas and raisins, 425g (15oz) glacé cherries, 275g (10oz) each mixed peel and flaked almonds, zest of 1 lemon, 1kg (2lb 6oz) plain flour, 2^1/$_2$ tsp each mixed spice and cinnamon, 950g (2lb 2oz) each softened butter and soft brown sugar, 17 medium eggs, beaten, 6 tbsp brandy.
Almond paste: 1.4kg (3lb)
Royal icing: 1.6kg (3^1/$_2$lb)

Madeira cake (quick mix method)

1 Preheat the oven to 170°C (150°C fan oven) mark 3. Grease and line a deep cake tin. Use the chart below to check the quantities you will need.

2 Sift the flours into a mixing bowl, add the butter, sugar, eggs and lemon juice or milk. Mix together with a wooden spoon, then beat for 1–2 minutes until smooth and glossy. Alternatively, use an electric mixer and beat for 1 minute only. Add any flavourings if required and mix until well blended.

3 Turn the mixture into the prepared tin and spread evenly. Give the tin a sharp tap to remove any air pockets. Make a depression in the centre of the mixture to ensure a level surface.

4 Bake in the centre of the oven following the baking times in the chart below as a guide, or until the cake springs back when lightly pressed in the centre.

5 Leave the cake to cool in the tin, then remove and cool completely on a wire rack. Wrap in clingfilm or foil and store in a cool place until required.

Madeira cake chart

CAKE TIN SIZE	20.5cm (8in) square 23cm (9in) round	23cm (9in) square 25.5cm (10in) round	25.5cm (10in) square 28cm (11in) round
Plain flour	225g (8oz)	250g (9oz)	275g (10oz)
Self-raising flour	225g (8oz)	250g (9oz)	275g (10oz)
Unsalted butter, softened	400g (14oz)	450g (1lb)	500g (1lb 2oz)
Caster sugar	400g (14oz)	450g (1lb)	500g (1lb 2oz)
Medium eggs	7	8	10
Lemon juice or milk	3½ tbsp	4 tbsp	4½ tbsp
Baking time (approx.)	1¾–2 hours	1¾–2 hours	2–2¼ hours

Splitting and filling a cake

Sponge cakes are often made in two tins, but can also be made in a deeper tin, then split and filled with jam, buttercream, cream or mascarpone with sliced fruit.

1 Allow the cake to cool completely before splitting.

2 Use a knife with a shallow thin blade, such as a ham knife, a bread knife or a carving knife. Cut a notch from top to bottom on one side of the cake so you will know where to line the pieces up after you've filled the cake. Cut midway between top and bottom, about 30 per cent of the way through the cake. Turn the cake while cutting, taking care to keep the blade parallel with the base, until you have cut all the way around.

3 Continue cutting until you have cut all the way through, then carefully lift off the top of the cake.

4 Warm jam slightly to make it easier to spread, or make sure buttercream is not too firm, then spread over the base, stopping 1cm (½in) from the edge.

5 Carefully put the top layer of cake on top of the filling and gently pat into place.

Apricot Glaze

Brush cakes with apricot glaze before covering with marzipan or with ready-to-roll icing (sugar paste). It can also be used to glaze fruit finishes on cakes and tarts. You will only need 3–4 tbsp at a time, but apricot glaze keeps well in the refrigerator, so it is worth making a larger quantity. Warm very gently before using.

To make 450g (1lb), you will need:
450g (1lb) apricot jam, 2 tbsp water.

1 Put the jam and water into a saucepan and heat gently, stirring occasionally, until melted.

2 Boil the jam rapidly for 1 minute, then strain through a sieve. Using a wooden spoon, rub through as much fruit as possible. Discard the skins left in the sieve.

3 Pour the glaze into a clean, hot jar, then seal with a clean lid and cool. Store in the refrigerator for up to two months.

Covering cakes

There are lots of options for covering cakes, depending on the finish you require. Marzipan gives an even, flat surface for covering with sugar paste or royal icing, particularly on fruit cakes. But if you want to avoid marzipan because of nut allergies, a Victoria sponge or Madeira cake can simply be covered with buttercream or apricot glaze, followed by a layer of ready–to–roll icing (sugar paste).

Cook's Tip

Ready-made icings, cake boards and a wide range of decorations are available from supermarkets and specialist cake decorating shops or via the internet.

Covering a cake with marzipan

Once you have applied the marzipan, you will need to allow time for it to dry before covering with icing. Home-made marzipan takes a little longer to dry out than the ready-made variety.

1 Trim the top of the cake level if necessary, then turn the cake over to give you a flat surface to work on. Place on the cake board, which should be at least 5cm (2in) larger than the cake. Brush the cake with apricot glaze (see page 25).

2 Dust the worksurface with sifted icing sugar, then roll out half the marzipan to fit the top of the cake. Lift the marzipan on top of the cake and smooth over, neatening the edges.

3 Cut a piece of string the same height as the cake with the marzipan topping, and another to fit around the diameter of the cake. Roll out the remaining marzipan and, using the string as a guide, trim the marzipan to size. Roll up the marzipan strip loosely. Place one end against the side of the cake and unroll the marzipan around the cake to cover it. Use a palette knife to smooth over the sides and joins of the marzipan.

4 Leave the cake in a cool, dry place to dry out thoroughly for at least 24 hours before covering with ready-to-roll icing. Allow to dry for at least two days before applying royal icing.

Covering a cake with ready-to-roll icing (sugar paste)

Ready-to-roll icing is pliable and can be used to cover cakes or moulded into decorative shapes. You can make your own (see below), but blocks of ready-to-roll icing (sugar paste) are available in a variety of colours from supermarkets and specialist cake decorating shops. A 450g (1lb) pack will cover an 18cm (7in) cake. Wrap any unused icing in clingfilm to stop it drying out and store in a cool, dry place.

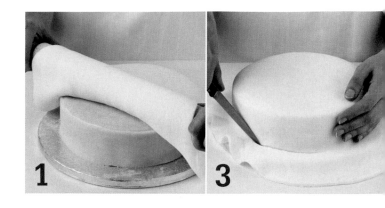

1 Dust the worksurface and rolling pin with sifted icing sugar. Knead the icing until pliable, then roll out into a round or square 5–7.5cm (2–3in) larger than the cake all round. Lift the icing on top of the cake and allow it to drape over the edges.

2 Dust your hands with sifted icing sugar and press the icing on to the sides of the cake, easing it down to the board.

3 Using a sharp knife, trim off the excess icing at the base to neaten. Reserve the trimmings to make decorations if required.

4 Using your fingers dusted with a little sifted icing sugar, gently rub the surface in a circular movement to buff the icing and make it smooth.

Home-made Sugar Paste

To make about 450g (1lb), enough to cover the top and sides of an 18cm (7in) round cake, you will need:
1 medium egg white, 1 tbsp liquid glucose, 500g (1lb 2oz) icing sugar, sifted, plus extra to dust.

1 Put the egg white and liquid glucose into a clean bowl, blending with a wooden spoon to break up the egg white. Add the icing sugar and mix until the icing begins to bind together. Knead with your fingers until the mixture forms a rough ball. Put the sugar paste on a surface lightly dusted with sifted icing sugar and knead thoroughly until smooth, pliable and free from cracks.

2 If the sugar paste is too soft to handle and is rather sticky, knead in some more sifted icing sugar until firm and pliable. If the sugar paste is dry and too firm, knead in a little boiled water until the paste becomes soft and pliable.

3 Wrap the sugar paste completely in clingfilm or store in a polythene bag with all the air excluded.

Covering a cake with royal icing or buttercream

Buttercream can be spread directly on to the cake; if you are using royal icing, first cover the cake with apricot glaze (see page 25).

1 Stir royal icing or buttercream just before using, to make sure it is easy to spread.

2 Put the cake on to a plate or cake board and use a palette knife to spread the icing evenly over the cake.

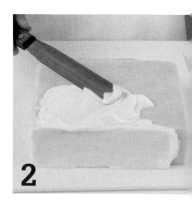

Hygiene

When you are preparing food, always follow these important guidelines:

Wash your hands thoroughly before handling food and again between handling different types of food, such as raw and cooked meat and poultry. If you have any cuts or grazes on your hands, be sure to keep them covered with a waterproof plaster.

Wash down worksurfaces regularly with a mild detergent solution or multi-surface cleaner.

Use a dishwasher if available. Otherwise, wear rubber gloves for washing-up, so that the water temperature can be hotter than unprotected hands can bear. Change drying-up cloths and cleaning cloths regularly. Note that leaving dishes to drain is more hygienic than drying them with a teatowel.

Keep raw and cooked foods separate, especially meat, fish and poultry. Wash kitchen utensils in between preparing raw and cooked foods. Never put cooked or ready-to-eat foods directly on to a surface that has just had raw fish, meat or poultry on it.

Keep pets out of the kitchen if possible; or make sure they stay away from worksurfaces. Never allow animals on to worksurfaces.

Food storage and hygiene

Storing food properly and preparing it in a hygienic way is important to ensure that food remains as nutritious and flavourful as possible, and to reduce the risk of food poisoning.

Shopping

Always choose fresh ingredients in prime condition from stores and markets that have a regular turnover of stock to ensure you buy the freshest produce possible.

Make sure items are within their 'best before' or 'use by' date. (Foods with a longer shelf life have a 'best before' date; more perishable items have a 'use by' date.)

Pack frozen and chilled items in an insulated cool bag at the check-out and put them into the freezer or refrigerator as soon as you get home.

During warm weather in particular, buy perishable foods just before you return home. When packing items at the check-out, sort them according to where you will store them when you get home – the refrigerator, freezer, storecupboard, vegetable rack, fruit bowl, etc. This will make unpacking easier – and quicker.

The storecupboard

Although storecupboard ingredients will generally last a long time, correct storage is important:

Always check packaging for storage advice – even with familiar foods, because storage requirements may change if additives, sugar or salt have been reduced. Check storecupboard foods for their 'best before' or 'use by' date and do not use them if the date has passed.

Keep all food cupboards scrupulously clean and make sure food containers and packets are properly sealed.

Once opened, treat canned foods as though fresh. Always transfer the contents to a clean container, cover and keep in the refrigerator. Similarly, jars, sauce bottles and cartons should be kept chilled after opening. (Check the label for safe storage times after opening.)

Transfer dry goods such as sugar, flour, rice and pasta to moisture-proof containers. When supplies are used up, wash the container well and thoroughly dry before refilling with new supplies.

Store oils in a dark cupboard away from any heat source as heat and light can make them turn rancid and affect their colour. For the same reason, buy olive oil in dark green bottles.

Store vinegars in a cool place; they can turn bad in a warm environment.

Store dried herbs, spices and flavourings in a cool, dark cupboard or in dark jars. Buy in small quantities as their flavour will not last indefinitely.

Refrigerator storage

Fresh food needs to be kept in the cool temperature of the refrigerator to keep it in good condition and discourage the growth of harmful bacteria. Store day-to-day perishable items, such as opened jams and jellies, mayonnaise and bottled sauces, in the refrigerator along with eggs and dairy products, fruit juices, bacon, fresh and cooked meat (on separate shelves), and salads and vegetables (except potatoes, which don't suit being stored in the cold). A refrigerator should be kept at an operating temperature of 4–5°C. It is worth investing in a refrigerator thermometer to ensure the correct temperature is maintained.

To ensure your refrigerator is functioning effectively for safe food storage, follow these guidelines:

To avoid bacterial cross-contamination, store cooked and raw foods on separate shelves, putting cooked foods on the top shelf. Ensure that all items are well wrapped.

Never put hot food into the refrigerator, as this will cause the internal temperature of the refrigerator to rise.

Avoid overfilling the refrigerator, as this restricts the circulation of air and prevents the appliance from working properly.

It can take some time for the refrigerator to return to the correct operating temperature once the door has been opened, so don't leave it open any longer than is necessary.

Clean the refrigerator regularly, using a specially formulated germicidal refrigerator cleaner. Alternatively, use a weak solution of bicarbonate of soda: 1 tbsp to 1 litre (1³/₄ pints) water.

If your refrigerator doesn't have an automatic defrost facility, defrost regularly.

Maximum refrigerator storage times

For pre-packed foods, always adhere to the 'use by' date on the packet. For other foods the following storage times should apply, providing the food is in prime condition when it goes into the refrigerator and that your refrigerator is in good working order:

Vegetables and Fruit

Green vegetables	3–4 days
Salad leaves	2–3 days
Hard and stone fruit	3–7 days
Soft fruit	1–2 days

Dairy Food

Cheese, hard	1 week
Cheese, soft	2–3 days
Eggs	1 week
Milk	4–5 days

Raw Meat

Bacon	7 days
Game	2 days
Minced meat	1 day
Offal	1 day
Poultry	2 days
Raw sliced meat	2 days

Cooked Meat

Sliced meat	2 days
Ham	2 days
Ham, vacuum-packed	1–2 weeks

(or according to the instructions on the packet)

1

Soups, Starters and Nibbles

Broad Bean, Pea and Mint Soup

1 tbsp olive oil

1 medium onion, finely chopped

1.1kg (2½lb) fresh broad beans
(pre-podded weight), podded

700g (1½lb) fresh peas (pre-podded weight), podded

1.1 litres (2 pints) hot vegetable stock

2 tbsp freshly chopped mint, plus extra sprigs to garnish

3 tbsp crème fraîche, plus extra to garnish (optional)

salt and ground black pepper

1 Heat the oil in a large pan and fry the onion gently for 15 minutes until softened.

2 Meanwhile, blanch the broad beans by cooking them for 2–3 minutes in a large pan of boiling water. Drain and refresh under cold water. Slip the beans out of their skins.

3 Put the beans and peas into the pan with the onion and stir for 1 minute. Add the hot stock and bring to the boil. Simmer for 5–8 minutes until the vegetables are tender, then cool for a few minutes. Stir in the mint, then whiz in batches in a blender or food processor until smooth. Alternatively, use a stick blender.

4 Return the soup to the rinsed-out pan, stir in the crème fraîche and check the seasoning. Reheat gently, then ladle into warmed bowls and garnish with a little crème fraîche, if you like, and a sprig of mint.

Serves 4	EASY		NUTRITIONAL INFORMATION	
	Preparation Time 20 minutes	**Cooking Time** 30 minutes	**Per Serving** 176 calories, 4g fat (of which 1g saturates), 22g carbohydrate, 0.1g salt	Vegetarian

Parsnip and Pear Soup

2 tbsp olive oil
1 large onion, roughly chopped
2 celery sticks, roughly chopped
1 garlic clove, crushed
1 tsp curry powder
$\frac{1}{2}$ tsp ground cumin
2 pinches hot chilli powder
450g (1lb) parsnips, roughly chopped
1 litre (1$\frac{3}{4}$ pints) hot vegetable stock
3 pears
15g ($\frac{1}{2}$oz) butter
1 tsp golden caster sugar
2 tbsp freshly chopped flat-leafed parsley to garnish (optional)

1 Heat the oil in a pan and add the onion, celery and garlic. Cover and cook gently for 10 minutes until softened. Stir in the spices and cook for 1 minute.

2 Add the parsnips and hot stock, cover and simmer for 10 minutes. Meanwhile, peel, core and chop two pears. Add to the pan and simmer, covered, for 5 minutes. Leave to cool a little, then whiz in a blender or food processor until smooth.

3 Peel and core the remaining pear, then slice thinly. Heat the butter in a pan and cook the pear for 3 minutes until lightly golden, then sprinkle the sugar over. Cook for 3 minutes, turning occasionally. Set aside.

4 Return the soup to the rinsed-out pan and reheat gently. Season to taste with salt and pepper, then ladle into warmed bowls and garnish with the caramelised pears and some parsley, if you like.

EASY		NUTRITIONAL INFORMATION		Serves
Preparation Time 25 minutes	**Cooking Time** 35 minutes	**Per Serving** 224 calories, 10g fat (of which 3g saturates), 32g carbohydrate, 0.2g salt	Vegetarian	**4**

Warm Chicken Liver Salad

75g (3oz) pinenuts
300g (11oz) asparagus tips, trimmed
450g (1lb) chicken livers
25g (1oz) butter
125g (4oz) wild rocket

For the orange and raisin dressing
6 small oranges
200ml (7fl oz) light olive oil
4 tbsp red wine vinegar
2 tbsp clear honey
50g (2oz) raisins
salt and ground black pepper

1 To make the dressing, grate the zest from 2 oranges, squeeze the juice and set aside. Peel and segment the remaining 4 oranges. Pour the oil and vinegar into a small pan. Add 6 tbsp of the orange juice (reserving the rest), the zest, honey and raisins. Season well with salt and pepper and whisk together. Bring gently to the boil, remove from the heat and set aside.

2 Put the pinenuts into a frying pan and heat gently to toast. Tip into a bowl to cool. Cook the asparagus for 5 minutes in simmering salted water. Drain, then dry on kitchen paper.

3 Cut off any sinew and fat from the livers, then pat dry on kitchen paper. Heat the butter in a large heavy-based pan and, when the foaming has subsided, add the livers and cook over a high heat for about 5 minutes or until well browned. Remove from the pan and keep warm.

4 Add the remaining orange juice and the dressing to the pan. Allow to bubble for 1–2 minutes, stirring and scraping the pan to dissolve any meat goodness.

5 Divide the livers, orange segments, asparagus and rocket among six bowls. Scatter the pinenuts on, spoon the dressing over, grind on some pepper and serve.

Serves 6	EASY		NUTRITIONAL INFORMATION	
	Preparation Time 10 minutes	**Cooking Time** 15–20 minutes	**Per Serving** 478 calories, 39g fat (of which 7g saturates), 14g carbohydrate, 0.3g salt	Gluten free

Get Ahead

Complete the recipe to the end of step 1.
To use Reheat the Stilton sauce gently just before serving. Complete the recipe.

200g (7oz) Stilton, crumbled

75ml (3fl oz) double cream

nutmeg to grate

a little milk

2 Cox's apples, cored and sliced

juice of $\frac{1}{2}$ lemon

1 head each green and red chicory

3 handfuls of watercress

50g (2oz) walnuts, toasted

salt and ground black pepper

Chicory, Stilton and Walnut Salad

1 Put 125g (4oz) Stilton into a pan with the cream and a grating of nutmeg. Stir over a gentle heat until bubbling. Thin with a little milk if too thick.

2 Toss the apples in the lemon juice in a bowl. Cut the chicory into bite-size pieces and add to the bowl with the watercress. Season with salt and pepper and toss. Divide among six plates along with the toasted walnuts and remaining Stilton. Drizzle the dressing over the salad and serve at once.

EASY		NUTRITIONAL INFORMATION		Serves
Preparation Time 15 minutes	**Cooking Time** 5 minutes	**Per Serving** 270 calories, 24g fat (of which 12g saturates), 5g carbohydrate, 0.8g salt	Vegetarian	**6**

Feta, Peach and Watercress Salad

3 slices walnut bread, cubed

1 tbsp olive oil

4 peaches, halved, stoned and cut into wedges

50g bag watercress

50g bag rocket

200g (7oz) feta cheese, roughly broken up

25g (1oz) each walnuts and mixed seeds (such as linseeds, pinenuts and sesame seeds)

1 tbsp toasted sesame oil

3 tbsp extra virgin olive oil

2 tbsp red wine vinegar

a few mint leaves, chopped

salt and ground black pepper

1 lemon, cut into six wedges, to serve

1 Preheat the oven to 200°C (180°C fan oven) mark 6. Put the cubed bread on a baking tray, drizzle with the olive oil and bake for 10 minutes until golden. Put the peaches into a large bowl with the watercress, rocket, feta and nuts and seeds.

2 Mix together the sesame and extra virgin olive oils and the vinegar, add the mint leaves and season with salt and pepper. Add half the dressing to the bowl and toss.

3 Divide the salad among six plates, then drizzle with the remaining dressing. Serve each with a lemon wedge to squeeze over.

EASY		NUTRITIONAL INFORMATION		Serves
Preparation Time 15 minutes	Cooking Time 10 minutes	Per Serving 271 calories, 22g fat (of which 7g saturates), 10g carbohydrate, 1.4g salt	Vegetarian	6

Get Ahead

Complete the recipe to the end of step 2 up to one day in advance.
To use Complete the recipe.

Smoked Fish Parcels with Dill and Beetroot Dressing

125g (4oz) smoked trout

1 tbsp horseradish sauce

2–3 tbsp crème fraîche

zest and juice of ¼ lemon

1½ tbsp freshly chopped dill, plus a few sprigs to garnish

8 large pieces of smoked salmon

4 balls of ready-cooked baby beetroot, diced

2 tsp cold-pressed rapeseed oil

salt and ground black pepper

lemon wedges and watercress to garnish

1 Break up the smoked trout into pieces and put into a food processor with the horseradish sauce, crème fraîche, lemon zest and juice. Whiz until blended. Transfer to a bowl, stir in 1 tbsp dill and check the seasoning.

2 Put one piece of smoked salmon on a board. Put a spoonful of trout mousse, about the size of a golf ball, in the centre. Fold up the smoked salmon to make a parcel, then turn over so the join is on the bottom. Repeat with the remaining mousse and salmon. Put on to a baking sheet, cover and chill for 30 minutes or until needed. Mix the remaining dill with the beetroot and oil.

3 Put a parcel in the middle of each plate and add the beetroot dressing. Garnish with a lemon wedge, watercress and a dill sprig and serve.

Serves 8	EASY		NUTRITIONAL INFORMATION	
	Preparation Time 20 minutes, plus chilling		**Per Serving** 143 calories, 8g fat (of which 3g saturates), 1g carbohydrate, 3.1g salt	Gluten free

Get Ahead

Complete the recipe to the end of step 3 up to one day in advance.
To use Complete the recipe.

Smoked Salmon and Watercress Breadsticks

350g (12oz) strong white flour
1½ tsp salt
½ x 7g packet fast-action dried yeast
40g (1½oz) Parmesan, grated
2 tbsp olive oil, plus extra for greasing
1 medium egg, beaten
1 tbsp poppy seeds
250g (9oz) smoked salmon
50g (2oz) watercress

1 Sift the flour into a large bowl and stir in the salt, yeast and Parmesan. Put 200ml (7fl oz) hand-hot water into a jug with the oil. Working quickly, add the wet ingredients to the flour and mix to a dough. Add a little extra water if it looks too dry. Tip out on to a work surface and knead for 5–10 minutes until smooth. Alternatively, put the ingredients into a freestanding mixer and knead until smooth.

2 Put into a lightly oiled bowl, cover with clingfilm and leave to rise in a warm place for 45 minutes.

3 Preheat the oven to 200°C (180°C fan oven) mark 6. Lightly oil two large baking sheets. Pinch off walnut-size pieces of dough and roll into thin 15cm (6in) lengths. Transfer to baking sheets. Brush with beaten egg and sprinkle with poppy seeds. Bake for 12–15 minutes until golden and cooked. Allow to cool on a wire rack.

4 Cut the salmon lengthways into slices. Hold pieces of watercress along the top of a breadstick and wrap a salmon slice around it. Arrange in glasses and serve.

EASY		NUTRITIONAL INFORMATION	Makes
Preparation Time 35 minutes, plus rising	**Cooking Time** 15 minutes	**Per Breadstick** 34 calories, 2g fat (of which 1g saturates), 1g carbohydrate, 0.4g salt	**30**

Blinis with Easy Butter Bean and Sweet Pepper Hummus

400g can butter beans
300g tub reduced-fat hummus
10 whole Peppadew sweet peppers
a handful of flat-leafed parsley
128g pack ready-made blinis
finely grated lemon zest

1 Drain the beans and whiz in a food processor with the hummus, sweet peppers and most of the parsley.

2 Spread the mixture on top of the blinis (you can freeze any leftover hummus for up to a month). Top with a little lemon zest and more chopped parsley and serve.

Serves 8	EASY	NUTRITIONAL INFORMATION	
	Preparation Time 10 minutes	Per Serving 160 calories, 8g fat (of which 1g saturates), 16g carbohydrate, 1.1g salt	Vegetarian

Cook's Tip

Prosciutto is Italian dry-cured ham. It is available from Italian delis and most supermarkets. Parma ham is a type of prosciutto, but other types are less expensive.

Cocktail Rolls

200g (7oz) smoked salmon slices

100g (3½oz) full-fat soft cheese or goat's cheese

1 tbsp dill-flavoured mustard or creamed horseradish

1 large courgette

about 2 tbsp hummus

200g (7oz) prosciutto (see Cook's Tip)

about 2 tbsp fruity chutney, such as mango

1 small bunch of chives, finely chopped

1 roasted red pepper, finely chopped

coarsely ground black pepper

1 Lay the smoked salmon on a sheet of greaseproof paper. Spread with a thin layer of cheese, then a layer of mustard or horseradish and roll up.

2 Using a vegetable peeler, pare the courgette into long, wafer-thin strips. Lay the strips on a board, spread with cheese, then hummus and roll up.

3 Lay the prosciutto on a board. Spread thinly with cheese, then with the chutney and roll up.

4 Stand the rolls on a greaseproof paper-lined baking sheet (trimming the bases if necessary), cover with clingfilm and chill for up to 8 hours.

5 About 2 minutes before serving, top each roll with a little cheese. Dip the salmon rolls into the chopped chives, the prosciutto rolls into the red pepper and the courgette rolls into the black pepper.

Serves 10	EASY	NUTRITIONAL INFORMATION	
	Preparation Time 20 minutes	**Per Serving** 117 calories, 7g fat (of which 3g saturates), 4g carbohydrate, 1.7g salt	Gluten free

Cook's Tip

Don't waste the flavoured oil left over from the olives. It's perfect for using in salad dressings and marinades.

Lemon and Rosemary Olives

a few fresh rosemary sprigs, plus extra to decorate

1 garlic clove

175g (6oz) mixed black and green Greek olives

zest of 1 lemon

2 tbsp vodka (optional)

300ml (½ pint) extra virgin olive oil

1 Put the rosemary and garlic into a small heatproof bowl and pour over enough boiling water to cover. Leave for 1–2 minutes, then drain well.

2 Put the olives, lemon zest and vodka, if using, in a glass jar and add the rosemary and garlic. Pour in enough oil to cover the olives, then cover and chill for at least 24 hours before using.

3 To serve, remove the olives from the oil and decorate with sprigs of fresh rosemary. Use within one week.

EASY	NUTRITIONAL INFORMATION		Serves
Preparation Time 15 minutes, plus at least 24 hours chilling	**Per Serving** 300 calories, 36g fat (of which 5g saturates), 0g carbohydrate, 1.2g salt	Vegetarian Gluten free • Dairy free	**6**

Mixed Italian Bruschetta

1 long thin French stick

400g can butter beans, drained and rinsed

a small handful of fresh mint, shredded

zest and juice of ½ lemon

2 tbsp extra virgin olive oil, plus extra to garnish

seeds from ½ pomegranate

150g (5oz) cherry tomatoes, quartered

200g (7oz) mozzarella bocconcini, halved

1 tbsp fresh basil pesto

2 tbsp fresh basil, chopped, plus extra leaves to garnish

a small handful of rocket

6 slices bresaola

15g (½oz) freshly shaved Parmesan

75g (3oz) roasted red pepper, sliced

2 tbsp black olive tapenade

1 Cut the bread diagonally into 24 slices and toast in batches. Mash together the butter beans, mint, lemon zest and juice and oil. Season to taste with salt and pepper and stir through most of the pomegranate seeds. Set aside.

2 In a separate bowl, stir together the cherry tomatoes, mozzarella bocconcini, pesto and basil.

3 To assemble, spoon the bean mixture on to six toasts and garnish with the remaining pomegranate seeds. Top a further six with the mozzarella mixture and six with rocket, bresaola and Parmesan. Drizzle with the oil. For the final six bruschetta, put a few slices of roasted pepper on each toast. Add a little tapenade and garnish with a basil leaf.

Serves 6	EASY	NUTRITIONAL INFORMATION
	Preparation Time 25 minutes	**Per Serving** 398 calories, 15g fat (of which 7g saturates), 47g carbohydrate, 2.5g salt

Cook's Tip

Chillies vary enormously in strength, from quite mild to blisteringly hot, depending on the type of chilli and its ripeness. Taste a small piece first to check it's not too hot for you.

Be extremely careful when handling chillies not to touch or rub your eyes with your fingers, or they will sting. Wash knives immediately after handling chillies. As a precaution, use rubber gloves when preparing them, if you like.

Squid with Haricot Beans and Rocket

450g (1lb) prepared squid, cut into thick rings

3 tbsp extra virgin olive oil

1 rosemary sprig, cut into four pieces

1 chilli, seeded and finely chopped (see Cook's Tip)

zest and juice of 1 lemon

2 x 400g cans haricot beans, drained and rinsed

2 tbsp olive oil

6 slices sourdough bread

55g pack rocket

salt and ground black pepper

lemon wedges to serve

1 Put the squid into a non-metallic bowl. Add 1 tbsp extra virgin olive oil, the rosemary, chilli and half the lemon zest. Season to taste with salt and pepper, then marinate for 30 minutes.

2 Put the beans into a large bowl with the remaining lemon zest, extra virgin olive oil and the lemon juice. Season and use a potato masher to pound into a rough purée.

3 Heat the olive oil in a wok or a non-stick frying pan and cook the squid for 1–2 minutes until opaque. Toast the bread.

4 Spread the bean purée over the toast. Top with the squid and rocket and serve with lemon wedges.

EASY		NUTRITIONAL INFORMATION	Serves
Preparation Time 20 minutes, plus marinating	**Cooking Time** about 2 minutes	**Per Serving** 317 calories, 12g fat (of which 2g saturates), 33g carbohydrate, 1.7g salt	**6**

2

Simple Midweek Suppers

Moules Marinière

2kg (4½lb) fresh mussels, scrubbed, rinsed and beards removed

25g (1oz) butter

4 shallots, finely chopped

2 garlic cloves, crushed

200ml (7fl oz) dry white wine

2 tbsp freshly chopped flat-leafed parsley

100ml (3½fl oz) single cream

salt and ground black pepper

crusty bread to serve

1 Tap the mussels on the worksurface and discard any that do not close or have broken shells. Heat the butter in a large non-stick lidded frying pan and sauté the shallots over a medium-high heat for about 10 minutes until soft.

2 Add the garlic, wine and half the parsley to the pan and bring to the boil. Tip in the mussels and reduce the heat a little. Cover and cook for about 5 minutes or until all the shells have opened; discard any mussels that don't open.

3 Lift out the mussels with a slotted spoon, put into serving bowls and cover with foil to keep warm. Add the cream to the stock, season with salt and pepper and cook for 1–2 minutes to heat through.

4 Pour a little sauce over the mussels and sprinkle with the rest of the parsley. Serve immediately with crusty bread.

EASY		NUTRITIONAL INFORMATION	Serves
Preparation Time 15 minutes	**Cooking Time** 20 minutes	**Per Serving** 262 calories, 13g fat (of which 7g saturates), 2g carbohydrate, 0.9g salt	**4**

Red Mullet with Cherry Tomatoes and Basil Oil

450g (1lb) cherry tomatoes, mixture of red and yellow

2 tbsp green peppercorns in brine, drained

8 garlic cloves, bruised not peeled

zest and juice of 1 small lemon

75ml (3fl oz) basil oil

12 x 50g (2oz) red mullet fillets, descaled

a small handful of fresh basil leaves

salt and ground black pepper

1 Preheat the oven to 180°C (160°C fan) mark 4. Halve the larger tomatoes, then put them all in a shallow roasting tin. Add the peppercorns, garlic and lemon zest, drizzle with half the oil and bake for 20 minutes.

2 Add the fish to the tin and drizzle with the remaining oil. Cook for a further 15–20 minutes until golden and cooked through.

3 Pour the lemon juice over the fish and sprinkle with basil leaves, salt and pepper. Serve with steamed new potatoes.

Serves 6	EASY		NUTRITIONAL INFORMATION	
	Preparation Time 10 minutes	Cooking Time about 40 minutes	Per Serving (without potatoes) 282 calories, 17g fat (of which 2g saturates), 4g carbohydrates, 0.4g salt	Dairy free

Gurnard with a Summer Vegetable Broth

3–4 tbsp plain flour
zest of 1 lemon
6 x 200g (7oz) gurnard fillets
25g (1oz) butter
1 tsp oil

For the vegetable broth

a handful each peas in their pods, runner beans and
baby leeks
1 tomato, seeded and chopped
18 cherry tomatoes
2 shallots, finely chopped
1 thyme sprig
1 bay leaf
450ml (¾ pint) light vegetable stock
leaves picked from 8 tarragon sprigs

1 Start the vegetable broth: pod the peas and put into a large bowl. Thickly slice the runner beans and leeks. Add both to the bowl with the chopped tomato and cherry tomatoes.

2 Put the flour on to a large plate. Add the lemon zest and season with salt and pepper. Toss the fish in the mixture and set aside.

3 Add the shallots to the pan and cook for 3–4 minutes until just golden. Add the thyme, bay leaf and stock and bring to the boil, then reduce the heat and simmer for 3–4 minutes.

4 Add the mixed vegetables. Roughly chop the tarragon leaves, add to the mixture and stir well, then cover and cook for 5 minutes until the vegetables are tender. Add the fish and cook gently for 3–4 minutes to heat through, then serve.

EASY		NUTRITIONAL INFORMATION	Serves
Preparation Time 20 minutes	**Cooking Time** about 20 minutes	**Per Serving** 483 calories, 26g fat (of which 13g saturates), 38g carbohydrate, 1.6g salt	**6**

1 litre (1³/₄ pints) chicken stock
½ tsp saffron
6 boneless, skinless chicken thighs
5 tbsp extra virgin olive oil
1 large onion, chopped
4 large garlic cloves, crushed
1 tsp paprika
2 red peppers, seeded and sliced
400g can chopped tomatoes
350g (12oz) long-grain rice
200ml (7fl oz) dry sherry
500g (1lb 2oz) cooked mussels
200g (7oz) cooked tiger prawns
juice of ½ lemon
salt and ground black pepper
lemon wedges and fresh flat-leafed parsley to serve

Simple Paella

1 Heat the stock, then add the saffron and leave to infuse for 30 minutes. Meanwhile, cut each chicken thigh into three pieces.

2 Heat half the oil in a large frying pan and, working in batches, fry the chicken for 3–5 minutes until pale golden brown. Set the chicken aside.

3 Lower the heat slightly and add the remaining oil. Fry the onion for 5 minutes or until soft. Add the garlic and paprika and stir for 1 minute. Add the chicken, red peppers and tomatoes.

4 Stir in the rice, then add one-third of the stock and bring to the boil. Season with salt and pepper.

5 Reduce the heat to a simmer and cook, uncovered, stirring continuously, until most of the liquid is absorbed.

6 Add the remaining stock a little at a time, letting it become absorbed into the rice before adding more. (This should take about 25 minutes.) Add the sherry and continue cooking for another 2 minutes – the rice should be quite wet, as it will continue to absorb liquid.

7 Add the mussels and prawns to the pan, including all their juices, with the lemon juice. Stir them in and cook for 5 minutes to heat through, then adjust the seasoning. Garnish with lemon wedges and fresh parsley and serve.

Serves 6	EASY		NUTRITIONAL INFORMATION
	Preparation Time 15 minutes, plus infusing	**Cooking Time** 50 minutes	**Per Serving** 554 calories, 16g fat (of which 3g saturates), 58g carbohydrate, 0.5g salt

Cook's Tip

Sage has a naturally strong, pungent taste, so you need only a little to flavour the chicken. Don't be tempted to add more than just one leaf to each chicken breast or it will overpower the finished dish.

Stuffed Chicken Breasts

vegetable oil to grease

150g (5oz) ball mozzarella

4 skinless chicken breasts, about 125g (4oz) each

4 sage leaves

8 slices Parma ham

new potatoes and spinach to serve

1 Preheat the oven to 200°C (180°C fan oven) mark 6. Lightly grease a baking sheet. Slice the mozzarella into eight, then put two slices on to each chicken piece. Top each with a sage leaf.

2 Wrap each piece of chicken in two slices of Parma ham, covering the mozzarella.

3 Put on to the prepared baking sheet and cook in the oven for 20 minutes or until the chicken is cooked through. Serve with new potatoes and spinach.

EASY		NUTRITIONAL INFORMATION		Serves
Preparation Time 5 minutes	**Cooking Time** 20 minutes	**Per Serving** 297 calories, 13g fat (of which 7g saturates), trace carbohydrate, 1.4g salt	Gluten free	**4**

Fennel Pork with Cabbage and Apple

2 tbsp olive oil

½ tbsp fennel seeds, crushed

1 tbsp freshly chopped sage

4 lean pork medallions, 125g (4oz) each

½ small red cabbage, shredded

450g (1lb) purple sprouting broccoli, tough ends removed

1 apple, cored and sliced into rings

salt and ground black pepper

1 Put 1 tbsp oil into a large shallow bowl. Add the fennel seeds and sage, season with salt and pepper and mix well. Add the pork and rub the mixture into the meat.

2 Heat the remaining oil in a wok or large frying pan and stir-fry the cabbage and broccoli for 6–8 minutes until starting to char.

3 Meanwhile, heat a non-stick griddle until hot and fry the pork for 2–3 minutes on each side until cooked through. Remove and set aside. Add the apple rings to the pan and griddle for 1–2 minutes on each side until starting to char and caramelise. Serve with the pork and vegetables.

Serves	EASY		NUTRITIONAL INFORMATION	
4	**Preparation Time** 10 minutes	**Cooking Time** 6–10 minutes	**Per Serving** 276 calories, 12g fat (of which 3g saturates), 9g carbohydrate, 0.3g salt	Gluten free Dairy free

Freezing Tip

To freeze Complete the recipe, transfer to a freezerproof container, cool, label and freeze for up to three months.
To use Thaw overnight at cool room temperature. Put into a pan, cover and bring to the boil, then reduce the heat to low and simmer until piping hot.

Quick Beef Stroganoff

700g (1½lb) rump or fillet steak, trimmed
50g (2oz) unsalted butter or 4 tbsp olive oil
1 onion, thinly sliced
225g (8oz) brown-cap mushrooms, sliced
3 tbsp brandy
1 tsp French mustard
200ml (7fl oz) crème fraîche
100ml (3½fl oz) double cream
3 tbsp freshly chopped flat-leafed parsley
salt and ground black pepper
rice or noodles to serve

1 Cut the steak into strips about 5mm (¼in) wide and 5cm (2in) long.

2 Heat half the butter or oil in a large heavy frying pan over a medium heat. Add the onion and cook gently for 10 minutes or until soft and golden. Remove with a slotted spoon and set aside. Add the mushrooms to the pan and cook, stirring, for 2–3 minutes until golden brown. Remove and set aside.

3 Increase the heat and quickly fry the meat, in two or three batches, for 2–3 minutes, stirring constantly to ensure even browning. Add the brandy and allow it to bubble to reduce.

4 Put the meat, onion and mushrooms back into the pan. Reduce the heat and stir in the mustard, crème fraîche and cream. Heat through, stir in most of the parsley and season with salt and pepper. Serve with rice or noodles, with the remaining parsley scattered over the top.

EASY		NUTRITIONAL INFORMATION		Serves
Preparation Time 10 minutes	**Cooking Time** 20 minutes	**Per Serving** 750 calories, 60g fat (of which 35g saturates), 3g carbohydrate, 0.5g salt	Gluten free • Dairy free	**4**

Chickpea and Chorizo Salad

3 tbsp red wine vinegar

2 tbsp extra virgin olive oil

1 garlic clove, crushed

zest and juice of 1 lemon

1½ x 400g cans chickpeas, drained and rinsed

125g (4oz) chorizo, skinned and diced

½ red onion, finely sliced

1 large red pepper, seeded and finely sliced

¼ cucumber, seeded and diced

3 tbsp each roughly chopped fresh mint, flat-leafed parsley and coriander

salt and ground black pepper

1 Mix together the vinegar, oil, garlic, lemon zest and juice in a large bowl.

2 Add the chickpeas, chorizo, onion, diced pepper and cucumber and season with salt and pepper.

3 Toss everything together, then add the herbs. Toss lightly again and serve.

Serves 4	EASY		NUTRITIONAL INFORMATION	
	Preparation Time 15 minutes		**Per Serving** 375 calories, 24g fat (of which 1g saturates), 26g carbohydrate, 2.2g salt	Dairy free

Get Ahead

Complete the recipe, without the garnish, and chill quickly. Keep in the refrigerator for up to two days.
To use Put into a pan, cover and bring to the boil, then simmer for 10–15 minutes. Complete the recipe.

Mauritian Vegetable Curry

3 tbsp vegetable oil

1 onion, finely sliced

4 garlic cloves, crushed

2.5cm (1in) piece of fresh root ginger, grated

3 tbsp medium curry powder

6 fresh curry leaves

150g (5oz) potato, peeled and cut into 1cm (½ in) cubes

125g (4oz) aubergine, cut into 2cm (1in) sticks, 5mm (¼ in) wide

150g (5oz) carrots, peeled and cut into 5mm (¼ in) dice

900ml (1½ pints) vegetable stock

pinch of saffron threads

1 tsp salt

ground black pepper

150g (5oz) green beans, trimmed

75g (3oz) frozen peas

3 tbsp freshly chopped coriander to garnish

1 Heat the oil in a large heavy-based pan over a low heat. Add the onion and fry for 5–10 minutes until golden. Add the garlic, ginger, curry powder and curry leaves and fry for a further minute.

2 Add the potato and aubergine to the pan and fry, stirring, for 2 minutes. Add the carrots, stock, saffron and salt and season with plenty of pepper. Cover and cook for 10 minutes until the vegetables are almost tender.

3 Add the beans and peas to the pan and cook for a further 4 minutes. Sprinkle with the chopped coriander and serve.

Serves 4	EASY		NUTRITIONAL INFORMATION	
	Preparation Time 15 minutes	**Cooking Time** 30 minutes	**Per Serving** 184 calories, 11g fat (of which 1g saturates), 18g carbohydrate, 1.7g salt	Vegetarian Gluten free • Dairy free

Calf's Liver with Fried Sage and Balsamic Vinegar

15g (1/2oz) butter, plus a little olive oil for frying

12 sage leaves

4 thin slices calf's liver

1–2 tbsp balsamic vinegar

rice, with freshly chopped parsley stirred through, or grilled polenta to serve

1 Preheat the oven to 130°C (110°C fan oven) mark 1/2. Melt the butter with a little oil in a heavy-based frying pan and when hot add the sage leaves. Cook briefly for 1 minute or so until crisp. Remove, put in a single layer in a shallow dish and keep warm in the oven.

2 Add a little extra oil to the pan, put in two slices of calf's liver and cook quickly for 30 seconds on each side over a high heat. Remove and put on a plate while you quickly cook the remaining two slices.

3 Put all four slices back into the pan, splash the balsamic vinegar over the top and cook for another minute or so. Top with the crispy sage leaves. Serve immediately with rice or polenta.

EASY		NUTRITIONAL INFORMATION		Serves
Preparation Time 5 minutes	**Cooking Time** 5 minutes	**Per Serving** 88 calories, 6g fat (of which 3g saturates), trace carbohydrate, 0.1g salt	Gluten free • Dairy free	4

Mushroom and Bean Hotpot

3 tbsp olive oil

700g (1½lb) chestnut mushrooms, roughly chopped

1 large onion, finely chopped

2 tbsp plain flour

2 tbsp mild curry paste

150ml (¼ pint) dry white wine

400g can chopped tomatoes

2 tbsp sun-dried tomato paste

2 x 400g cans mixed beans, drained and rinsed

3 tbsp mango chutney

3 tbsp roughly chopped fresh coriander and mint

1 Heat the oil in a large pan over a low heat, then fry the mushrooms and onion until the onion is soft and dark golden. Stir in the flour and curry paste and cook for 1–2 minutes.

2 Add the wine, tomatoes, sun-dried tomato paste and beans and bring to the boil, then simmer gently for 30 minutes or until most of the liquid has reduced. Stir in the chutney and herbs before serving.

Serves	EASY		NUTRITIONAL INFORMATION	
6	**Preparation Time** 15 minutes	**Cooking Time** 30 minutes	**Per Serving** 280 calories, 10g fat (of which 1g saturates), 34g carbohydrate, 1.3g salt	Vegetarian Dairy free

Cook's Tips

Mint Sauce: finely chop 20g (³⁄₄oz) fresh mint and mix with 1 tbsp each olive oil and white wine vinegar.
Garlic-infused Oil: gently heat 2 tbsp olive oil with peeled, sliced garlic for 5 minutes and use immediately. Do not store.

Lamb Chops with Crispy Garlic Potatoes

2 tbsp mint sauce (see Cook's Tips)
8 small lamb chops
3 medium potatoes, peeled and cut into 5mm (¹⁄₄in) slices
2 tbsp garlic-infused olive oil (see Cook's Tips)
1 tbsp olive oil
salt and ground black pepper
steamed green beans to serve

1 Spread the mint sauce over the lamb chops and leave to marinate while you prepare the potatoes.

2 Boil the potatoes in a pan of lightly salted water for 2 minutes or until just starting to soften. Drain, tip back into the pan, season with salt and pepper and toss with the garlic oil.

3 Meanwhile, heat the olive oil in a large frying pan and fry the chops for 4–5 minutes on each side until just cooked, adding a splash of boiling water to the pan to make a sauce. Remove the chops and sauce from the pan and keep warm.

4 Add the potatoes to the pan and fry over a medium heat for 10–12 minutes until crisp and golden. Divide the potatoes, chops and sauce among four plates and serve with green beans.

EASY		NUTRITIONAL INFORMATION		Serves
Preparation Time 10 minutes	**Cooking Time** 20 minutes	**Per Serving** 835 calories, 45g fat (of which 19g saturates), 22g carbohydrate, 0.7g salt	Gluten free • Dairy free	**4**

3

Special Suppers

Get Ahead

Complete the recipe to the end of step 3, up to 3 hours in advance. Wrap in clingfilm and chill.
To use Complete the recipe.

Cook's Tip

Some pastry brands come in different sizes. If yours does, trim to make a dozen 18 x 28cm (7 x 11in) rectangles. If you have any left over, wrap in clingfilm and freeze for up to one month.

Spicy Salmon Parcels with Ginger Butter

75g (3oz) unsalted butter, at room temperature

2.5cm (1in) piece fresh root ginger, peeled and grated

zest of ½ lemon

175g (6oz) chilled filo pastry (see Cook's Tip)

6 x 125g (4oz) salmon fillets, skinned (remove tiny bones with tweezers if you have time)

1 each small red and green chilli, seeded and finely chopped (see page 45)

salt and ground black pepper

steamed broccoli to serve

1 Mix 50g (2oz) butter with the ginger and lemon zest, then season with salt and pepper. Wrap in clingfilm, roll into a sausage and chill until firm.

2 Preheat the oven to 200°C (180°C fan oven) mark 6. Melt the remaining butter in a small pan. Brush a sheet of filo with a little melted butter, keeping the other sheets covered with a damp tea towel while you work. Put another sheet on top and brush with butter. Put a salmon fillet in the middle and sprinkle over one-sixth of the chilli. Season with black pepper.

3 Unwrap the ginger butter and slice into six rounds. Top the salmon with a slice of butter, then gather the filo around the fish to make a parcel. Transfer to a non-stick baking sheet and brush with the remaining melted butter. Repeat to make six parcels.

4 Cook for 15–18 minutes until the pastry is crisp and golden. Serve immediately with broccoli.

Serves 6	EASY		NUTRITIONAL INFORMATION
	Preparation Time 25 minutes	**Cooking Time** 15–18 minutes	**Per Serving** 414 calories, 27g fat (of which 10g saturates), 18g carbohydrate, 0.6g salt

Tarragon Chicken with Fennel

1 tbsp olive oil
4 chicken thighs
1 onion, finely chopped
1 fennel bulb, finely chopped
juice of ½ lemon
200ml (7fl oz) hot chicken stock
200ml (7fl oz) crème fraîche
a small bunch of tarragon, roughly chopped
salt and ground black pepper

1 Preheat the oven to 200°C (180°C fan oven) mark 6. Heat the oil in a large flameproof casserole over a medium to high heat. Add the chicken thighs and fry for 5 minutes or until browned, then remove and set aside to keep warm.

2 Add the onion to the pan and fry for 5 minutes, then add the fennel and cook for 5–10 minutes until softened.

3 Add the lemon juice to the pan, followed by the hot stock. Bring to a simmer and cook until the sauce is reduced by half.

4 Stir in the crème fraîche and put the chicken back into the pan. Stir once to mix, then cover and cook in the oven for 25–30 minutes. Stir the tarragon into the sauce, season with salt and pepper and serve.

EASY		NUTRITIONAL INFORMATION		Serves
Preparation Time 10 minutes	**Cooking Time** 45–55 minutes	**Per Serving** 334 calories, 26g fat (of which 15g saturates), 3g carbohydrate, 0.5g salt	Gluten free	**4**

Cook's Tip

Beurre manié is a mixture of equal parts of softened butter and flour that has been kneaded together to form a paste. It's used to thicken sauces and stews. It's whisked in towards the end of cooking, then boiled briefly to allow it to thicken.

Coq au Vin

750ml bottle full-bodied white wine, such as Burgundy or Chardonnay

4 tbsp brandy

2 bouquet garni (fresh parsley and thyme sprigs, 1 bay leaf and a piece of parsley)

1 garlic clove, bruised

flour to coat

1 chicken, about 1.4kg (3lb), jointed, or 2 boneless breasts, halved, plus 2 drumsticks and 2 thighs

125g (4oz) butter

125g (4oz) rindless unsmoked bacon rashers, cut into strips

225g (8oz) baby onions, peeled with root ends intact

225g (8oz) brown-cap mushrooms, halved, or quartered if large

salt and ground black pepper

buttered noodles or rice to serve

For the beurre manié

25g (1oz) butter mixed with 25g (1oz) plain flour

1 Preheat the oven to 180°C (160°C fan oven) mark 4. Pour the wine and brandy into a pan and add 1 bouquet garni and the garlic. Bring to the boil and simmer until reduced by half. Allow to cool.

2 Season the flour with salt and pepper and use to coat the chicken joints lightly. Melt half the butter in a large frying pan. When foaming, add the chicken joints and brown all over (in batches if necessary). Transfer to a flameproof casserole. Add the bacon to the frying pan and fry until golden. Remove with a slotted spoon and add to the chicken.

3 Strain the cooled, reduced wine mixture over the chicken and add the other bouquet garni. Bring to the boil, cover and cook in the oven for 30 minutes.

4 Meanwhile, melt the remaining butter in a frying pan and fry the onions until tender and lightly browned. Add the mushrooms and fry until softened.

5 Add the onions and mushrooms to the casserole, cover and cook for a further 10 minutes or until the chicken is tender. Lift out the chicken and vegetables with a slotted spoon and put into a warmed serving dish. Cover and keep warm.

6 Bring the cooking liquid in the casserole to the boil. Whisk in the beurre manié, a piece at a time, until the sauce is shiny and syrupy. Check the seasoning.

7 Pour the sauce over the chicken and serve with buttered noodles or rice.

EASY		NUTRITIONAL INFORMATION	Serves
Preparation Time 45 minutes	**Cooking Time** about 1 hour	**Per Serving** 787 calories, 51g fat (of which 22g saturates), 24g carbohydrate, 1.5g salt	**4**

Get Ahead

Complete the recipe to the end of step 2, then store the duck in the fridge, covered in clingfilm, for up to 24 hours.
To use Bring to room temperature before completing the recipe.
You can also make the sauce in advance and reheat with the juices from the rested duck.

Duck with Port and Figs

4 x 200g (7oz) duck breasts, fat of each breast scored diagonally, making sure you don't cut into the meat, and sinew and excess fat trimmed

1 tsp rapeseed oil

150ml (¼ pint) port

300ml (½ pint) hot chicken stock

zest of 1 orange, plus 1–2 tbsp orange juice

9 fresh figs, halved

mixed vegetables to serve

1 Preheat the oven to 200°C (180°C fan oven) mark 6. Put the duck, skin side down, with the oil into a large frying pan set over the lowest heat to let the fat run out. This will take 15–20 minutes (see Get Ahead). Pour the fat into a bowl and use to cook roast potatoes later. When the skin has turned golden and most of the fat has drained out, put the duck breasts on a rack set in a roasting tin, skin-side up. Cook the duck in the oven for 15 minutes for pink and 20 minutes for well done. Cover loosely with foil and leave to rest while you make the sauce.

2 Put the port, hot stock and orange zest into the frying pan. Bubble rapidly until syrupy and reduced by two-thirds. Stir in orange juice to taste and any juices from the duck. Season to taste and keep warm.

3 Heat a griddle pan over a medium-high heat and griddle the figs cut-side down for 3 minutes until softened. Slice the duck breasts diagonally or leave whole and arrange on warmed plates with the figs. Drizzle the sauce over and serve with vegetables.

Serves	EASY		NUTRITIONAL INFORMATION	
6	**Preparation Time** 15 minutes	**Cooking Time** 45 minutes	**Per Serving** 758 calories, 58g fat (of which 16g saturates), 37g carbohydrate, 0.4g salt	Dairy free

Freezing Tip

To freeze Complete the recipe to the end of step 4, without the garnish. Put in a freezerproof container, cool and freeze for up to three months.
To use Thaw overnight at cool room temperature. Preheat the oven to 180°C (160°C fan oven) mark 4. Bring to the boil on the hob, cover tightly and reheat in the oven for about 30 minutes or until piping hot.

Braised Beef with Pancetta and Mushrooms

175g (6oz) smoked pancetta or smoked streaky bacon, cubed
2 leeks, trimmed and thickly sliced
1 tbsp olive oil
450g (1lb) braising steak, cut into 5cm (2in) pieces
1 large onion, finely chopped
2 carrots, thickly sliced
2 parsnips, thickly sliced
1 tbsp plain flour
300ml (½ pint) red wine
1–2 tbsp redcurrant jelly
125g (4oz) chestnut mushrooms, halved
ground black pepper
freshly chopped flat-leafed parsley to garnish

1 Preheat the oven to 170°C (150°C fan oven) mark 3. Fry the pancetta or bacon in a shallow flameproof casserole for 2–3 minutes until golden. Add the leeks and cook for a further 2 minutes or until they are just beginning to colour. Remove with a slotted spoon and set aside.

2 Heat the oil in the casserole. Fry the beef in batches for 2–3 minutes until golden brown on all sides. Remove and set aside. Add the onion and fry over a gentle heat for 5 minutes or until golden. Stir in the carrots and parsnips and fry for 1–2 minutes.

3 Put the beef back into the casserole and stir in the flour to soak up the juices. Gradually add the wine and 300ml (½ pint) water, then stir in the redcurrant jelly. Season with pepper and bring to the boil. Cover with a tight-fitting lid and cook in the oven for 2 hours.

4 Stir in the leeks, pancetta and mushrooms, cover and cook for a further 1 hour or until everything is tender. Serve hot, sprinkled with chopped parsley.

EASY		NUTRITIONAL INFORMATION		Serves
Preparation Time 20 minutes	**Cooking Time** about 3½ hours	**Per Serving** 541 calories, 25g fat (of which 9g saturates), 30g carbohydrate, 1.6g salt	Dairy free	**4**

Braised Guinea Fowl and Red Cabbage

2 tbsp rapeseed oil

2 oven-ready guinea fowl

150g (5oz) smoked lardons

400g (14oz) whole shallots, peeled

1 small red cabbage, cored and finely sliced

12 juniper berries, crushed

2 tsp dark brown sugar

1 tbsp red wine vinegar

2 fresh thyme sprigs

150ml (¼ pint) hot chicken stock

1 Preheat the oven to 180°C (160°C fan oven) mark 4. Heat 1 tbsp oil in a flameproof casserole large enough for both birds and brown the guinea fowl over a medium to high heat. Remove from the casserole and set aside.

2 Add the remaining oil to the casserole with the lardons. Fry gently to release the fat, then add the shallots and cook over a medium heat until lightly browned.

3 Stir in the red cabbage and cook for 5 minutes, stirring, until the cabbage has softened slightly. Add the juniper berries, sugar, vinegar, thyme and hot stock. Season with salt and pepper.

4 Put the guinea fowl on top of the cabbage mixture, then cover the casserole tightly with a lid or double thickness of foil and braise in the oven for 1½ hours. Remove the lid and continue cooking for 30 minutes until the birds are cooked through – the juices should run clear when you pierce the thighs with a skewer.

5 Transfer the guinea fowl to a board and spoon the cabbage and juices on to a serving platter. Keep warm. Joint the birds into eight, as you would a chicken, then arrange the guinea fowl on the platter on top of the cabbage. Serve at once.

Serves 8	EASY		NUTRITIONAL INFORMATION	
	Preparation Time 30 minutes	**Cooking Time** 2 hours 20 minutes	**Per Serving without lime butter** 373 calories, 17g fat (of which 6g saturates), 12g carbohydrate, 0.9g salt	Dairy free

Cook's Tips

Tapenade is made from black olives, capers, garlic and olive oil.

The marinade is ideal for other cuts of lamb, such as steaks or fillets, or spread over a boned shoulder or leg.

Lamb with Tapenade

6 tbsp olive oil

4 tbsp ready-made tapenade

2 tbsp Pernod or Ricard

2 garlic cloves, crushed

8 loin lamb chops, each about 125g (4oz)

ground black pepper

grilled sliced fennel and courgettes, and lemon halves to serve

1 Mix together the oil, tapenade, Pernod or Ricard and the garlic, then rub into the lamb chops and season with black pepper. Leave to marinate for at least 30 minutes or overnight.

2 Preheat the barbecue or griddle. Cook the chops for 4–5 minutes on each side. Serve with lightly grilled fennel and courgette slices and lemon halves to squeeze over.

EASY		NUTRITIONAL INFORMATION		Serves
Preparation Time 5 minutes, plus minimum 30 minutes marinating	**Cooking Time** 8–10 minutes	**Per Serving** 579 calories, 34g fat (of which 15g saturates), 0g carbohydrate, 0.4g salt	Gluten free • Dairy free	**4**

Belly of Pork with Cider and Rosemary

2kg (4½lb) piece pork belly roast, preferably on the bone

500ml bottle medium cider

600ml (1 pint) hot chicken stock

20g pack fresh rosemary

3 fat garlic cloves, halved

2 tbsp olive oil

zest and juice of 1 large orange and 1 lemon

1½ tsp salt

3 tbsp light muscovado sugar

1 tbsp plain flour

25g (1oz) softened butter

roasted vegetables to serve

1 Preheat the oven to 150°C (130°C fan oven) mark 2. Put the pork, skin-side up, into a roasting tin just large enough to hold it. Add the cider, hot stock and half the rosemary. Bring to the boil on the hob, then cover with foil and cook in the oven for 4 hours. Leave to cool in the cooking liquid.

2 Strip the leaves from the remaining rosemary stalks and chop. Put into a pestle and mortar with the garlic, oil, orange and lemon zest, 1 tsp salt and 1 tbsp muscovado sugar. Pound for 3–4 minutes to make a rough paste. Alternatively, use a strong bowl and the end of a rolling pin.

3 Remove the pork from the tin, reserving the cooking liquid, and slice off the skin from the top layer of fat. Set aside. Score the fat into a diamond pattern. Cover loosely with clingfilm and chill until required.

4 Pat the pork rind dry with kitchen paper and transfer it (fat-side up) to a foil-lined baking sheet. Cook under a hot grill, about 10cm (4in) away from the heat, for 5 minutes. Turn over, sprinkle lightly with salt, then grill for 7–10 minutes or until crisp. Cool, then cut into rough pieces. Store in an airtight container.

5 Strain the cooking liquid into a pan. Add the orange and lemon juice and the remaining sugar, bring to the boil and bubble until reduced by half. Meanwhile, blend the flour and butter to a paste, then whisk into the bubbling liquid. Boil for 4–5 minutes until thickened. Set aside.

6 When almost ready to serve, preheat the oven to 220°C (200°C fan oven) mark 7. Cook the pork uncovered in a roasting tin for 20 minutes until piping hot. Wrap the crackling in foil and warm in the oven for the last 5 minutes of the cooking time. Heat the gravy on the hob. Take the meat to the table, carve the pork and serve with the crackling by the side and roasted vegetables.

Serves 8	EASY		NUTRITIONAL INFORMATION
	Preparation Time 30 minutes, plus chilling	**Cooking Time** 4¾ hours	**Per Serving** 671 calories, 49g fat (of which 17g saturates), 9g carbohydrate, 1.1g salt

Try Something Different

Replace the feta with sliced mozzarella, or smoked mozzarella. Mix some olive oil with the crushed garlic, brush over the mozzarella and stack up in step 3.

Aubergine, Feta and Tomato Stacks

200g (7oz) feta cheese, crumbled
2 tbsp olive oil, plus extra to brush
1 garlic clove, crushed, plus 1 garlic clove for rubbing
2 plump aubergines, cut into 1cm (½ in) thick slices
a handful of fresh basil leaves, torn
3 large vine-ripened tomatoes, each sliced into four
salt and ground black pepper
rocket and toasted ciabatta to serve

1 Preheat the barbecue or grill. Put the feta into a bowl, stir in the oil and garlic, season with salt and pepper and set aside.

2 Brush each aubergine slice with a little oil and barbecue or grill for about 6 minutes, turning occasionally until softened and golden. Remove from the heat.

3 Sprinkle a little of the feta mixture on to six of the aubergine slices, put some torn basil leaves on top, then a slice of tomato. Season well. Repeat with the feta mixture, basil leaves, aubergine and tomato. Finish with an aubergine slice and press down firmly.

4 Secure each stack with a cocktail stick. Either use a hinged grill rack, well oiled, or wrap the stacks in foil and barbecue for 2–3 minutes on each side. Serve with rocket leaves and toasted ciabatta rubbed with a garlic clove.

Serves 4	EASY		NUTRITIONAL INFORMATION	
	Preparation Time 10 minutes	**Cooking Time** 12 minutes	**Per Serving** 138 calories, 11g fat (of which 5g saturates), 4g carbohydrate, 1.2g salt	Vegetarian Gluten free

Smoked Haddock Risotto with Poached Eggs

200g (7oz) smoked haddock

50g (2oz) butter

1 large leek, white part only, trimmed and finely sliced

150ml (¼ pint) dry white wine

300g (11oz) arborio rice

1.1 litres (2 pints) hot chicken stock

4 large eggs

salt and ground black pepper

1 tbsp freshly chopped parsley to garnish

1 Put the haddock into a dish, pour boiling water over, cover and leave for 10 minutes. Flake the fish into bite-size pieces, discarding the skin and the bones.

2 Melt half the butter in a heavy-based pan. Add the leek and cook gently, stirring occasionally, for 15 minutes until softened. Add the wine and boil rapidly until it has almost evaporated. Add the rice and cook, for 1 minute, stirring to coat the grains.

3 Put the hot stock into a pan and bring to the boil, then keep at a gentle simmer. Add a ladleful of the hot stock to the rice. Simmer, stirring, until all the liquid has been absorbed. Continue adding the stock, a ladleful at a time, until the rice is tender but still has some bite – this will take about 20 minutes and you may not need to add all the stock.

4 Meanwhile, bring a wide shallow pan of water to the boil. Crack an egg into a cup, turn off the heat under the pan and slip in the egg close to the water. Repeat with the other eggs and cover the pan. Leave to stand for 3 minutes.

5 Before adding the last ladleful of stock, stir in the pieces of fish and the remaining butter and check the seasoning. Heat the risotto through, adding the remaining stock if necessary. Remove the eggs with a slotted spoon and trim. Top each serving of risotto with a poached egg and a sprinkling of parsley.

EASY		NUTRITIONAL INFORMATION	Serves 4
Preparation Time 15 minutes	**Cooking Time** about 40 minutes	**Per Serving** 508 calories, 17g fat (of which 8g saturates), 61g carbohydrate, 1.4g salt	

500g pack puff pastry, thawed if frozen

25g (1oz) butter

2 shallots, finely chopped

200g (7oz) button mushrooms, finely chopped

1 tbsp redcurrant jelly

650g (1lb 7oz) venison loin

6 slices Parma ham

1 medium egg, beaten

50g (2oz) blueberry conserve

50ml (2fl oz) each hot chicken stock and red wine

salt and ground black pepper

Venison Wellington

1 Preheat the oven to 200°C (180°C fan oven) mark 6. Roll out a third of the pastry into a rectangle measuring 5cm (2in) wider on all sides than the venison. Prick the pastry all over with a fork, then cover and chill for 15 minutes.

2 Melt half the butter in a large frying pan and fry the shallots gently for 5 minutes to soften slightly. Add the mushrooms. Cook on a high heat for 5 minutes, stir in the jelly and season with salt and pepper. Leave to cool. Bake the pastry on a baking sheet for 15–20 minutes until golden. Cool on a wire rack.

3 Season the venison. Heat the remaining butter in a frying pan and brown the meat all over. Set aside to cool.

4 Arrange the slices of Parma ham on a board, each slightly overlapping another, in a rectangle large enough to cover the venison. Spread the mushroom mix over the ham and put the venison on top. Wrap the ham tightly around the meat. Put the baked pastry rectangle on a baking sheet and top with the wrapped venison.

5 Roll out the remaining pastry so it's large enough to cover the meat and tuck under the pastry base. Brush the border of cooked pastry with beaten egg, then cover with raw pastry. Trim the edges, reserving any spare pastry. Brush the Wellington with beaten egg. Roll out any trimmings and cut out letters to spell 'venison'. Put on top of Wellington, brush with egg and chill for 30 minutes.

6 Preheat the oven to 200°C (180°C fan oven) mark 6. Brush the Wellington again with beaten egg and bake for 25–30 minutes until deep golden.

7 To make the sauce, simmer the blueberry conserve, hot stock and wine in a pan for 10 minutes. Serve warm with slices of the Wellington.

Serves 8	EASY		NUTRITIONAL INFORMATION
	Preparation Time 45 minutes, plus chilling	**Cooking Time** 1 hour	**Per Serving** 304 calories, 19g fat (of which 2g saturates), 30g carbohydrate, 0.9g salt

Get Ahead

Complete the recipe up to 24 hours in advance. Cool in the tin, cover and keep chilled.
To use To serve hot, turn out the tortilla, slice and lay flat on a lightly greased baking sheet. Cover with foil and reheat in a hot oven for 10–15 minutes.

Sweet Potato and Goat's Cheese Tortilla

2 large sweet potatoes, peeled and thinly sliced

3 tbsp olive oil

3 peppers (mixed red and yellow), seeded and roughly chopped

1 fennel bulb, thinly sliced

3 garlic cloves, crushed

1 small onion, thinly sliced

3 medium eggs

284ml carton single cream

125g (4oz) each fresh soft goat's cheese and Taleggio cheese, chopped

75g (3oz) young spinach leaves, watercress leaves or fresh basil

salt and ground black pepper

1 Preheat the oven to 220°C (200°C fan oven) mark 7. Put the potatoes into a large roasting tin, season with salt and pepper and drizzle with half the oil. Toss well. Put the peppers, fennel, garlic and onion into a second tin. Season, drizzle with the remaining oil and toss well. Put both tins into the oven and roast for 30–35 minutes or until the vegetables are tender.

2 Whisk together the eggs, cream and cheese and season with plenty of coarsely ground black pepper.

3 Line the base and sides of a 20.5cm (8in) round, 7.5cm (3in) deep cake tin with non-stick baking parchment.

4 Reduce the oven temperature to 170°C (150°C fan oven) mark 3. Layer the roasted vegetables in the tin with the spinach, watercress or basil, adding a little egg mix as you go. Pour in any remaining egg mix and cook the tortilla in the centre of the oven for about 1 hour 15 minutes or until the egg is set and the top golden. Serve warm or cold.

EASY			NUTRITIONAL INFORMATION		Serves
Preparation Time 15 minutes	**Cooking Time** 1 hour 50 minutes		**Per Serving** 316 calories, 22g fat (of which 11g saturates), 20g carbohydrate, 0.7g salt	Vegetarian	**8**

4

Family Celebrations

Roasted Salmon

3 lemons, 2 sliced and the juice of ¹/₂, plus extra lemon slices to garnish

2 salmon sides, filleted, each 1.4kg (3lb), skin on, boned and trimmed

2 tbsp dry white wine

salt and ground black pepper

cucumber slices and 2 large bunches of watercress to garnish

For the dressing

500g carton crème fraîche

500g carton natural yogurt

2 tbsp horseradish sauce

3 tbsp freshly chopped tarragon

4 tbsp capers, roughly chopped, plus extra to garnish

¹/₄ cucumber, seeded and finely chopped

1 Preheat the oven to 190°C (170°C fan oven) mark 5. Take two pieces of foil, each large enough to wrap one side of salmon, and put a piece of greaseproof paper on top. Divide the lemon slices between each piece of greaseproof paper and lay the salmon on top, skin side up. Season with salt and pepper, then pour the lemon juice and wine over.

2 Score the skin of each salmon fillet at 4cm (1¹/₂in) intervals to mark 10 portions. Scrunch the foil around each fillet, keeping it loose so the fish doesn't stick. Cook for 25 minutes until the flesh is just opaque. Unwrap the foil and cook for a further 5 minutes until the skin is crisp. Leave the fish to cool quickly in a cold place. Re-wrap and chill.

3 Put all the dressing ingredients into a bowl and season with salt and pepper. Mix well, then cover and chill.

4 Serve the salmon on a platter garnished with lemon and cucumber slices and watercress. Garnish the dressing with capers and chopped cucumber and serve separately.

Cook's Tips

There'll be a lot of hot liquid in the parcel of salmon, so ask someone to help you lift it out of the oven.

To check the fish is cooked, ease a knife into one of the slashes in the skin. The flesh should look opaque and the knife should come out hot.

To prepare ahead Complete the recipe to the end of step 3, then keep the salmon wrapped and chilled for up to one day. Complete the recipe.

EASY		NUTRITIONAL INFORMATION		Serves
Preparation Time 20 minutes, plus cooling and chilling	**Cooking Time** about 30 minutes	**Per Serving** 366 calories, 27g fat (of which 10g saturates), 3g carbohydrate, 0.4g salt	Gluten free	**20**

Get Ahead

Complete the recipe to the end of step 1, then cover
and chill for up to two days.
To use Complete the recipe.

Mediterranean Salmon

12 x 125g (4oz) salmon fillets, skinned

5 tbsp ready-made pesto

50g (2oz) sun-dried tomatoes, chopped

100g (3½oz) black olives

3 lemons

new potatoes and a green salad to serve

1 Mix the salmon, pesto, tomatoes and olives in a large
bowl. Sprinkle with the zest of 1 lemon, then cover
and chill for 30 minutes.

2 Preheat the oven to 200°C (180°C fan oven) mark 6.
Arrange the salmon in a large ovenproof serving dish
and spoon the tomatoes, olives and pesto marinade
over.

3 Cut each of the remaining lemons into six wedges
and put around the salmon. Cook for 10–12 minutes
or until the fish flakes when pushed with a knife,
then serve with potatoes and salad.

Serves	EASY		NUTRITIONAL INFORMATION	
12	**Preparation Time** 15 minutes, plus marinating	**Cooking Time** 10–12 minutes	**Per Serving** 251 calories, 18g fat (of which 3g saturates), 1g carbohydrate, 0.8g salt	Gluten free

Get Ahead

Complete the recipe, then cool and chill in a freezerproof container for up to two days, or freeze for up to a month.
To use Allow to come to room temperature, or thaw overnight at cool room temperature. Return to the casserole pan, cover and reheat gently until hot. Add a little stock or water if it looks dry.

Spring Lamb Casserole

3 tbsp olive oil

1.1kg (2½lb) boneless shoulder of spring lamb, chopped into 4cm (1½in) cubes – remove excess fat and gristle

500ml (17fl oz) hot vegetable stock

1 tsp each smoked paprika, ground cinnamon and coriander

2 rosemary sprigs

2 large onions, each cut into 12–14 wedges

300g (11oz) Chantenay carrots, trimmed

125g (4oz) dried apricots, roughly chopped

300ml (½ pint) dry white wine

2 x 410g tins chickpeas, drained and rinsed

mixed green vegetables to serve

1 Heat half the oil in a large flameproof ovenproof casserole and brown the lamb pieces in batches. Set aside in a bowl.

2 Pour a little of the hot stock into the pan. Scrape the bottom with a wooden spoon to release any sticky goodness, then pour over the reserved lamb. Heat the remaining oil in the pan and stir in the spices, rosemary, onions, carrots and apricots. Cook for 1 minute.

3 Stir in the wine, remaining stock and half the chickpeas, then return the lamb to the pan. Cover and bring to the boil. Turn the heat down and simmer for 1 hour 30 minutes stirring occasionally, until the lamb is tender.

4 Meanwhile, mash the remaining chickpeas. Stir into the finished casserole and check the seasoning. Remove the rosemary stalks and serve with vegetables.

EASY		NUTRITIONAL INFORMATION		Serves
Preparation Time 30 minutes	**Cooking Time** about 1¾ hours	**Per Serving** 307 calories, 15g fat (of which 5g saturates), 18g carbohydrate, 0.5g salt	Dairy free	**12**

Luxury Smoked Fish Pie

1.1kg (2½lb) Desirée potatoes, peeled and cut into rough chunks

450ml (¾ pint) milk

125g (4oz) butter

125g (4oz) Cheddar, grated

75ml (2½fl oz) dry white wine

150ml (¼ pint) fish stock

450g (1lb) skinless smoked haddock fillet, undyed if possible, cut into wide strips

350g (12oz) skinless salmon fillet, cut into wide strips

40g (1½oz) plain flour

75ml (2½fl oz) double cream

1 tbsp capers, drained, rinsed and chopped

1½ tbsp freshly chopped flat-leafed parsley

2 medium eggs, hard-boiled

salt and ground black pepper

1 Preheat the oven to 180°C (160°C fan oven) mark 4. Put the potatoes into a pan of salted water, bring to the boil, cover and simmer until tender.

2 Warm 100ml (3½fl oz) milk. Drain the potatoes, then put back into the pan over a low heat for 2 minutes. Mash until smooth. Stir in 75g (3oz) butter, half the cheese and the warmed milk, then season with salt and pepper. Cover and set aside.

3 Meanwhile, bring the wine, stock and remaining milk to the boil in a large wide pan. Add the haddock and salmon. Return the liquid to the boil, then reduce the heat to poach the fish gently for 5 minutes or until it flakes easily. Lift the fish with a draining spoon into a 1.4 litre (2½ pint) deep ovenproof dish and flake with a fork if necessary. Put the cooking liquid to one side.

4 Melt the remaining butter in another pan, add the flour and stir until smooth, then cook for 2 minutes. Gradually add the fish liquid, whisking until smooth. Bring to the boil, stirring, and cook for 2 minutes or until thickened. Stir in the cream, capers and parsley and season to taste with salt and pepper.

5 Shell the eggs and chop roughly. Scatter over the fish, then pour the sauce over. Spoon the potato mixture on top. Sprinkle with the remaining cheese.

6 Bake the pie for 35–40 minutes until golden and bubbling at the edges. Serve hot.

Freezing Tip

Double the ingredient quantities and make two pies, each to serve four people, then freeze one for another day. **Complete the recipe** to the end of step 4. Cool the sauce quickly, then complete step 5. Freeze for up to three months. **To use** Thaw overnight at cool room temperature. Bake at 190°C (170°C fan oven) mark 5 for 50–60 minutes until golden and bubbling at the edges.

Serves 4	EASY		NUTRITIONAL INFORMATION
	Preparation Time 30 minutes	**Cooking Time** 1 hour 20 minutes	**Per Serving** 1057 calories, 63g fat (of which 34g saturates), 66g carbohydrate, 3.8g salt

175g (6oz) ready-to-eat dried peaches or apricots
400ml (14fl oz) unsweetened apple juice
grated zest and juice of 1 small orange
175ml (6fl oz) extra virgin olive oil
3 tbsp freshly chopped flat-leafed parsley
1 tbsp freshly chopped chives
1.8kg (4lb) loin of pork, boned
1.1kg (2½lb) potatoes
6–8 fresh rosemary sprigs, leaves stripped
1 tbsp plain flour
salt and ground black pepper
carrots to serve

Roast Pork with Peaches

1 Soak the dried peaches or apricots in half the apple juice overnight.

2 Drain the fruit (keep the juice) and put into a food processor, then chop roughly. Add the orange zest, 4 tbsp oil and the herbs and mix together, then season with salt and pepper.

3 If the pork has crackling, remove it carefully with a sharp knife, lay it in a small roasting tin, rub lightly with 1 tbsp oil and sprinkle with salt. Set aside.

4 Place the pork, fat-side up, on a board, then split it almost in half by slicing horizontally through the eye of the meat towards the fatty side. Open it like a book, spread the fruit stuffing on the bottom half and reshape. Tie with string and set aside.

5 Preheat the oven to 200°C (180°C fan oven) mark 6. Cut the potatoes into wedges and boil for 1–2 minutes; drain, reserving the water. Return the potatoes to the pan over a low heat to dry them off.

Toss in the remaining oil with the rosemary leaves and season. Put into a roasting tin and roast for 20–30 minutes.

6 Put the pork on a rack over the potatoes and spoon the reserved apple juice over it. Put the crackling on the shelf above the pork. Cook for a further 1¼–1½ hours, basting from time to time, until the pork is cooked and the crackling is crisp. Put the pork, crackling and potatoes on a serving plate and keep warm.

7 Add the flour to the juices in the roasting tin. Put the tin on the hob and stir for 1–2 minutes over a medium heat until smooth. Pour in the orange juice, remaining apple juice and potato water, then bring to the boil and simmer for 3–4 minutes until slightly thickened.

8 Slice the pork and crackling, strain the gravy and serve with the pork, potatoes and carrots.

Serves 8	EASY		NUTRITIONAL INFORMATION	
	Preparation Time 1 hour, plus overnight soaking	**Cooking Time** 1 hour 50 minutes, plus resting	**Per Serving** 617 calories, 40g fat (of which 12g saturates), 37g carbohydrate, 0.2g salt	Dairy free

Butternut Squash and Spinach Lasagne

1 butternut squash, peeled, halved, seeded and cut into 3cm (1¼in) cubes

2 tbsp olive oil

1 onion, sliced

25g (1oz) butter

25g (1oz) plain flour

600ml (1 pint) milk

250g (9oz) ricotta cheese

1 tsp freshly grated nutmeg

225g bag baby leaf spinach

6 'no need to pre-cook' lasagne sheets

50g (2oz) pecorino cheese or Parmesan, freshly grated

salt and ground black pepper

1 Preheat the oven to 200°C (180°C fan oven) mark 6. Put the squash into a roasting tin with the oil, onion and 1 tbsp water. Mix well and season with salt and pepper. Roast for 25 minutes, tossing halfway through.

2 To make the sauce, melt the butter in a pan, then stir in the flour and cook over a medium heat for 1–2 minutes. Gradually add the milk, stirring constantly. Reduce the heat to a simmer and cook, stirring, for 5 minutes or until the sauce has thickened. Crumble the ricotta into the sauce and add the nutmeg. Mix together thoroughly and season with salt and pepper.

3 Heat 1 tbsp water in a pan. Add the spinach, cover and cook until just wilted. Season generously.

4 Spoon the squash mixture into a 1.7 litre (3 pint) ovenproof dish. Layer the spinach on top, then cover with a third of the sauce, then the lasagne. Spoon the remaining sauce on top, season and sprinkle with the grated cheese. Cook for 30–35 minutes until the cheese topping is golden and the pasta is cooked.

EASY		NUTRITIONAL INFORMATION		Serves
Preparation Time 30 minutes	Cooking Time about 1 hour	Per Serving 273 calories, 17g fat (of which 7g saturates), 18g carbohydrate, 0.6g salt	Vegetarian	6

Cook's Tip

Home-cooked ham is great hot or cold, but cooking a large joint is often impractical. Roasting two medium joints at the same time means you can serve a hot joint and have plenty left to eat cold.

Maple, Ginger and Soy-roasted Gammon

2 x 2.5kg (5½lb) smoked boneless gammon joints

8 tbsp vegetable oil

7.5cm (3in) piece fresh root ginger, peeled and grated

8 tbsp maple syrup

6 tbsp dark soy sauce

12 star anise (optional)

1 If the gammon is salty (check with your butcher), soak it in cold water overnight. Alternatively, bring to the boil in a large pan of water and simmer for 10 minutes, then drain.

2 Preheat the oven to 200°C (180°C fan oven) mark 6. Put the joints into a roasting tin and pour 4 tbsp oil over them. Cover with foil and roast for 1 hour 50 minutes or 20 minutes per 450g (1lb).

3 Mix together the ginger, maple syrup, soy sauce and remaining oil in a bowl.

4 Take the gammon out of the oven, remove the foil and allow to cool a little, then carefully peel away the skin and discard. Score the fat in a criss-cross pattern, stud with the star anise, if using, then pour the ginger sauce over the gammon. Continue to roast for another 20 minutes or until the glaze is golden brown. Slice and serve one joint warm. Cool the other, wrap in foil and chill until needed.

Serves	EASY		NUTRITIONAL INFORMATION	
18	**Preparation Time** 10 minutes	**Cooking Time** 2 hours 10 minutes	**Per Serving** 392 calories, 21g fat (of which 7g saturates), 2g carbohydrate, 6.1g salt	Dairy free

Get Ahead

Complete the recipe to the end of step 4. Cool quickly and chill for up to 24 hours.
To use Bring the lamb to room temperature. Complete the recipe.

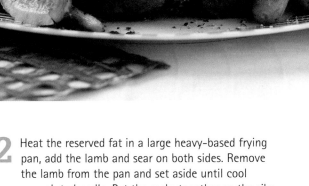

Guard of Honour with Hazelnut and Herb Crust

2 trimmed racks of lamb
salt and ground black pepper
roasted root vegetables to serve

For the hazelnut and herb crust

75g (3oz) fresh breadcrumbs made from Italian bread, such as ciabatta
2 tbsp each freshly chopped flat-leafed parsley and thyme
1 tbsp freshly chopped rosemary
2 garlic cloves, crushed
2 tbsp olive oil
50g (2oz) hazelnuts, toasted and roughly chopped
4 tbsp Dijon mustard

1 Preheat the oven to 200°C (180°C fan oven) mark 6. Trim off as much of the fat from the lamb as possible and set aside. Season the lamb well with pepper.

2 Heat the reserved fat in a large heavy-based frying pan, add the lamb and sear on both sides. Remove the lamb from the pan and set aside until cool enough to handle. Put the racks together so the ribs interlock. Place the lamb in a roasting tin, rib bones uppermost, with the lamb fat. Roast for 10 minutes.

3 Meanwhile, make the hazelnut crust. Combine the breadcrumbs, herbs, garlic, oil and seasoning for 30 seconds in a food processor, then add the hazelnuts and pulse for a further 30 seconds.

4 Remove the lamb from the oven. Spread the fatty side with the mustard. Press the hazelnut crust on to the mustard. Baste the lamb with the fat in the roasting tin and put back into the oven for 15–20 minutes for rare, 20–25 minutes for medium-rare and 25–30 minutes for well done. When cooked, remove from the oven, cover with foil and leave in a warm place for 10 minutes before carving. Arrange the lamb on a serving dish. Serve with roasted root vegetables.

EASY		NUTRITIONAL INFORMATION		Serves
Preparation Time 30 minutes	**Cooking Time** 25–35 minutes, plus resting	**Per Serving** 488 calories, 39g fat (of which 15g saturates), 11g carbohydrate, 1.2g salt	Dairy free	**6**

Classic Roast Beef with Yorkshire Puddings

1 boned and rolled rib, sirloin, rump or topside of beef, about 1.8kg (4lb)

1 tbsp plain flour

1 tbsp mustard powder

salt and ground black pepper

fresh thyme sprigs to garnish

Yorkshire puddings and vegetables to serve

For the gravy

150ml (¼ pint) red wine

600ml (1 pint) beef stock

Cook's Tip

Yorkshire Puddings: sift 125g (4oz) plain flour and ½ tsp salt into a bowl. Mix in 150ml (¼ pint) milk, then add 2 medium eggs, beaten, and season with pepper. Beat until smooth, then whisk in another 150ml (¼ pint) milk. Pour about 3 tbsp fat from the beef roasting tin and use to grease 8–12 individual Yorkshire pudding tins. Put the tins into a preheated oven at 220°C (200°C fan oven) mark 7 for 5 minutes or until the fat is almost smoking. Pour the batter into the tins. Bake for 15–20 minutes until well risen, golden and crisp. Serve immediately.

1 Preheat the oven to 230°C (210°C fan oven) mark 8. Put the beef into a roasting tin, with the thickest part of the fat uppermost. Mix the flour with the mustard powder, salt and pepper and rub the mixture over the beef.

2 Roast the beef in the middle of the oven for 30 minutes.

3 Baste the beef and turn the oven down to 190°C (170°C fan oven) mark 5. Cook for a further 1 hour, approximately, basting occasionally. Meanwhile, prepare the Yorkshire pudding batter (see Cook's Tip).

4 Put the beef on to a warmed carving dish, cover loosely with foil and leave to rest in a warm place. Increase the oven temperature to 220°C (200°C fan oven) mark 7 and cook the Yorkshire puddings.

5 Meanwhile, make the gravy. Skim off any remaining fat from the roasting tin. Put the tin on the hob, add the wine and boil until syrupy. Pour in the stock and, again, boil until syrupy; there should be about 450ml (¾ pint) gravy. Taste and adjust the seasoning.

6 Carve the beef into slices. Garnish with thyme and serve with the gravy, Yorkshire puddings and vegetables of your choice.

Serves 4	EASY		NUTRITIONAL INFORMATION
	Preparation Time 20 minutes	**Cooking Time** about 1½ hours, plus resting	**Per Serving** 510 calories, 24g fat (of which 9g saturates), 16g carbohydrate, 0.5g salt

Get Ahead

Complete the recipe to the end of step 5, cool quickly, cover and chill for up to two days.
To use Bring the pheasant to the boil and reheat in the oven at 180°C (160°C fan) mark 4 for 20–25 minutes.

Pheasant with Cider and Apples

2 pheasants, each weighing about 700g (1½lb), each cut into four portions

2 tbsp plain flour, plus extra to dust

50g (2oz) butter

4 rashers streaky bacon

225g (8oz) onions, roughly chopped

275g (10oz) celery, roughly chopped

4 eating apples, such as Granny Smith, cored, cut into large pieces and tossed in 1 tbsp lemon juice

1 tbsp dried juniper berries, lightly crushed

2.5cm (1in) piece fresh root ginger, peeled and finely chopped

300ml (½ pint) chicken stock

2 x 440ml cans dry cider

142ml carton double cream

salt and ground black pepper

fried apple wedges, thyme sprigs and juniper berries to garnish

1 Preheat the oven to 170°C (150°C fan) mark 3. Season each pheasant portion and dust lightly with flour. Melt the butter in a large flameproof casserole and brown the pheasant pieces in batches until deep golden brown. Remove and keep warm.

2 Put the bacon into the casserole and cook for 2–3 minutes or until golden. Add the onions, celery, apples, juniper and ginger and cook for 8–10 minutes. Stir the flour into the vegetables and cook for 2 minutes, then add the stock and cider and bring to the boil. Return the pheasant to the casserole, cover and cook in the oven for 45 minutes–1 hour or until tender.

3 Lift the pheasant out of the sauce and keep it warm. Strain the sauce through a sieve and return it to the casserole with the cream. Bring to the boil and bubble for 10–15 minutes or until syrupy. Return the pheasant to the sauce and season.

4 To serve, garnish the pheasant with the fried apple wedges, thyme sprigs and juniper berries.

Serves 8	EASY		NUTRITIONAL INFORMATION
	Preparation Time 1 hour	**Cooking Time** 1 hour	**Per Serving** 463 calories, 27g fat (of which 13g saturates), 13g carbohydrate, 0.7g salt

Freezing Tip

To freeze Complete the recipe to the end of step 3, cool, cover and freeze for up to one month.

To use Cook from frozen for 45 minutes, then unwrap the foil slightly and cook for a further 15 minutes until turning golden.

40g (1½oz) butter, plus extra for greasing

1 onion, finely chopped

1 garlic clove, crushed

225g (8oz) mixed white nuts, such as brazils, macadamias, pinenuts and whole almonds, ground in a food processor

125g (4oz) fresh white breadcrumbs

grated zest and juice of ½ lemon

75g (3oz) sage Derby cheese or vegetarian Parmesan, grated

125g (4oz) cooked, peeled (or vacuum-packed) chestnuts, roughly chopped

½ x 400g can artichoke hearts, drained and roughly chopped

1 medium egg, lightly beaten

2 tsp each freshly chopped parsley, sage and thyme, plus extra sprigs

salt and ground black pepper

White Nut Roast

1 Preheat the oven to 200°C (180°C fan oven) mark 6. Melt the butter in a pan and cook the onion and garlic for 5 minutes or until soft. Put into a large bowl and set aside to cool.

2 Add the nuts, breadcrumbs, lemon zest and juice, cheese, chestnuts and artichokes. Season well and bind together with the egg. Stir in the herbs.

3 Put the mixture on to a large piece of buttered foil and shape into a fat sausage, packing tightly. Scatter with the extra herb sprigs and wrap in the foil.

4 Cook on a baking sheet for 35 minutes, then unwrap the foil slightly and cook for a further 15 minutes until turning golden. Slice and serve

EASY		NUTRITIONAL INFORMATION		Serves 8
Preparation Time 20 minutes	**Cooking Time** about 1 hour	**Per Serving** 371 calories, 28g fat (of which 9g saturates), 20g carbohydrate, 0.8g salt	Vegetarian	

Cook's Tip

Red Wine Sauce: soften 350g (12oz) shallots, finely chopped, in 2 tbsp olive oil for 5 minutes. Add 3 garlic cloves, chopped, and 3 tbsp tomato purée and cook for 1 minute, then add 2 tbsp balsamic vinegar. Simmer briskly until reduced to almost nothing, then add 200ml (7fl oz) red wine and reduce by half. Pour in 600ml (1 pint) beef stock and simmer until reduced by one-third.

Fillet of Beef en Croûte

1–1.4kg (2¼–3lb) fillet of beef, trimmed

50g (2oz) butter

2 shallots, chopped

15g (½oz) dried porcini mushrooms, soaked in 100ml (3½fl oz) boiling water

2 garlic cloves, chopped

225g (8oz) flat mushrooms, finely chopped

2 tsp freshly chopped thyme, plus extra sprigs to garnish

175g (6oz) chicken liver pâté

175g (6oz) thinly sliced Parma ham

375g ready-rolled puff pastry

1 medium egg, beaten

salt and ground black pepper

Red Wine Sauce (see Cook's Tip) to serve

1 Season the beef with salt and pepper. Melt 25g (1oz) butter in a large frying pan and, when foaming, add the beef and cook for 4–5 minutes to brown all over. Transfer to a plate and leave to cool.

2 Melt the remaining butter in a pan, add the shallots and cook for 1 minute. Drain the porcini mushrooms, reserving the liquid, and chop them. Add them to the pan with the garlic, the reserved liquid and the fresh mushrooms. Turn up the heat and cook until the liquid has evaporated, then season with salt and pepper and add the thyme. Leave to cool.

3 Put the chicken liver pâté in a bowl and beat until smooth. Add the mushroom mixture and stir well. Spread half the mushroom mixture evenly over one side of the fillet. Lay half the Parma ham on a length of clingfilm, overlapping the slices. Invert the mushroom-topped beef on to the ham. Spread the remaining mushroom mixture on the other side of the beef, then lay the rest of the Parma ham, also overlapping, on top of the mushroom mixture. Wrap the beef in the clingfilm to form a firm sausage shape and chill for 30 minutes. Preheat the oven to 220°C (200°C fan oven) mark 7.

4 Cut off one-third of the pastry and roll out on a lightly floured surface to 3mm (⅛in) thick and 2.5cm (1in) larger all round than the beef. Prick all over with a fork. Transfer to a baking sheet and bake for 12–15 minutes until brown and crisp. Leave to cool, then trim to the size of the beef and place on a baking sheet. Remove the clingfilm from the beef, brush with the egg and place on the cooked pastry.

5 Roll out the remaining pastry to a 25.5 x 30.5cm (10 x 12in) rectangle. Roll a lattice pastry cutter over it and gently ease the lattice open. Cover the beef with the lattice, tuck the ends under and seal the edges. Brush with the beaten egg, then cook for 40 minutes for rare to medium, 45 minutes for medium. Leave to rest for 10 minutes before carving. Garnish with thyme and serve with Red Wine Sauce.

EASY		NUTRITIONAL INFORMATION	Serves
Preparation Time 1 hour, plus soaking and chilling	**Cooking Time** about 1 hour 20 minutes, plus resting	**Per Serving** 1090 calories, 72g fat (of which 21g saturates), 36g carbohydrate, 3.6g salt	**4**

Freezing Tip

To freeze Complete the recipe and leave to cool. Return the tart to the tin, wrap well and freeze for up to one month.

To use Thaw at cool room temperature, then warm through for 15 minutes in an oven preheated to 200°C (180°C fan oven) mark 6.

Leek and Fennel Tart

275g (10oz) plain flour

125g (4oz) butter, chilled and cut into cubes

75g (3oz) vegetarian Parmesan, finely grated

1 tbsp sunflower oil

2 large leeks – about 200g (7oz) – trimmed and chopped

525g (1lb 3oz) fennel, chopped

3 medium eggs, plus 2 yolks

200ml (7fl oz) each milk and double cream

1½ tbsp poppy seeds

a few thyme sprigs, leaves stripped and stalks discarded

salt and ground black pepper

1 Pulse the flour and butter in a processor until they resemble breadcrumbs. Tip into a bowl and stir in 40g (1½oz) Parmesan, then 75ml (3fl oz) cold water until the dough comes together. Knead lightly, form into a ball, wrap in clingfilm and chill for 30 minutes.

2 Heat the oil in a large pan, add the leeks and fennel, then cover and cook over a low heat for 15–20 minutes until soft. Strain off liquid. Leave to cool.

3 Preheat the oven to 200°C (180°C fan oven) mark 6. Roll out the pastry and line a 30.5cm (12in) loose-bottomed fluted tart tin. Prick the base, cover with greaseproof paper and fill with baking beans. Chill for 10 minutes. Bake for 12–15 minutes. Remove beans and paper. Bake for 8–10 minutes. If pastry puffs up, push it down. Reduce oven to 170°C (150°C fan oven) mark 3. Mix the eggs, yolks, milk, cream, poppy seeds and remaining Parmesan. Season. Spoon leek mixture into the pastry case. Pour in the egg mixture, sprinkle with thyme and cook for 40–45 minutes until set. Remove outside of tin but leave tart on the base to cool.

Serves	EASY		NUTRITIONAL INFORMATION	
12	**Preparation Time** 35 minutes, plus chilling	**Cooking Time** 1¼–1½ hours	**Per Serving** 319 calories, 24g fat (of which 13g saturates), 20g carbohydrate, 0.5g salt	Vegetarian

Get Ahead

Complete the recipe to the end of step 4 up to one day in advance. Cover and keep in the fridge for up to 24 hours.
To use Complete the recipe.

Red Onion Tarte Tatin

50g (2oz) butter

2 tbsp olive oil

1.1kg (2½lb) red onions, sliced into rounds

1 tbsp light muscovado sugar

175ml (6fl oz) white wine

4 tsp white wine vinegar

1 tbsp freshly chopped thyme, plus extra to garnish (optional)

450g (1lb) puff pastry

plain flour to dust

salt and ground black pepper

1 Lightly grease two 23cm (9in) non-stick sandwich tins with a little of the butter and set aside.

2 Melt the remaining butter with the oil in a large non-stick frying pan. Add the onions and sugar and fry for 10–15 minutes or until golden, keeping the onions in their rounds.

3 Preheat the oven to 220°C (200°C fan) mark 7. Add the wine, vinegar and thyme to the pan. Bring to the boil, and let it bubble until the liquid has evaporated. Season with salt and pepper, then divide the mixture between the tins and leave to cool.

4 Halve the pastry. On a lightly floured surface, roll out each piece thinly into a round shape just larger than the sandwich tin. Put one pastry round over the onion mixture in each tin and tuck in the edges. Prick the pastry dough all over with a fork.

5 Cook the tarts for 15–20 minutes or until the pastry is risen and golden. Take out of the oven and put a large warm plate over the pastry. Turn over and shake gently to release the tart, then remove the tin. Scatter with thyme, if you like, and cut into wedges to serve.

EASY		NUTRITIONAL INFORMATION		Serves
Preparation Time 15 minutes	**Cooking Time** 35–40 minutes	**Per Serving** 235 calories, 15g fat (of which 3g saturates), 23g carbohydrate, 0.4g salt	Vegetarian	**12**

Get Ahead

Complete the recipe to the end of step 4, then cover and chill overnight until ready to cook.
To use Complete the recipe.

Wild Mushroom Pithiviers

450g (1lb) wild mushrooms
300ml (½ pint) milk
200ml (7fl oz) double cream
2 garlic cloves, crushed
450g (1lb) floury potatoes, peeled and thinly sliced
freshly grated nutmeg
50g (2oz) butter
2 tsp freshly chopped thyme, plus fresh sprigs to garnish
flour to dust
2 x 500g packs puff pastry, thawed if frozen
1 large egg, beaten
salt and ground black pepper

1 Rinse the mushrooms in cold running water to remove any grit, then pat dry with kitchen paper. Roughly slice.

2 Put the milk and cream into a large heavy-based pan with the garlic. Bring to the boil, then add the potatoes. Bring back to the boil, then simmer gently, stirring occasionally, for 15–20 minutes until the potatoes are tender. Season with salt, pepper and nutmeg and leave to cool.

3 Melt the butter in a large frying pan. When it's sizzling, add the mushrooms and cook over a high heat, stirring all the time, for 5–10 minutes until the mushrooms are cooked and the juices have evaporated completely. Season. Stir in the chopped thyme, then set aside to cool.

4 On a lightly floured surface, roll out the pastry thinly. Cut into eight rounds, approximately 12.5cm (5in) in diameter, for the tops and eight rounds, approximately 11.5cm (4½in) in diameter, for the bases. Put the smaller pastry rounds on baking sheets and brush the edges with beaten egg. Put a large spoonful of the cooled potato mixture in the centre of each round, leaving a 1cm (½in) border around the edge. Top with a spoonful of the mushroom mixture, then cover with the pastry tops. Press the edges together well to seal. Chill for 30 minutes–1 hour.

5 Meanwhile, preheat the oven to 220°C (200°C fan oven) mark 7 and put two baking trays in to heat up. Use the back of a knife to scallop the edges of the pastry and brush the top with the remaining beaten egg. If you like, use a knife to decorate the tops of the pithiviers.

6 Put the pithiviers, on their baking sheets, on the preheated baking trays. Cook for 15–20 minutes until deep golden brown, swapping the trays around in the oven halfway through cooking. Serve immediately, garnished with thyme sprigs.

Serves 8	EASY		NUTRITIONAL INFORMATION	
	Preparation Time 1 hour, plus 1 hour chilling and cooling	**Cooking Time** about 1 hour	**Per Serving** 710 calories, 51g fat (of which 12g saturates), 58g carbohydrate, 1.2g salt	Vegetarian

5

Sweet Treats

Quick Gooey Chocolate Puddings

100g (3½oz) butter, plus extra to grease

100g (3½oz) golden caster sugar, plus extra to dust

100g (3½oz) plain chocolate (at least 70% cocoa solids), broken into pieces

2 large eggs

20g (¾oz) plain flour

icing sugar to dust

whipped cream to serve (optional)

1 Preheat the oven to 200°C (180°C fan oven) mark 6. Butter four 200ml (7fl oz) ramekins and dust with sugar. Melt the chocolate and butter in a heatproof bowl over a pan of gently simmering water. Take the bowl off the pan and leave to cool for 5 minutes.

2 Whisk the eggs, caster sugar and flour together in a bowl until smooth. Fold in the chocolate mixture and pour into the ramekins.

3 Stand the dishes on a baking tray and bake for 12–15 minutes until the puddings are puffed and set on the outside, but still runny inside. Turn out, dust with icing sugar and serve immediately with whipped cream, if you like.

EASY		NUTRITIONAL INFORMATION		Serves
Preparation Time 15 minutes	**Cooking Time** 12–15 minutes	**Per Serving** 468 calories, 30.6g fat (of which 18.5g saturates), 46.2g carbohydrate, 0.6g salt	Vegetarian	4

Summer Pudding

800g (1lb 12oz) mixed summer berries,
such as 250g (9oz) each redcurrants and blackcurrants
and 300g (11oz) raspberries

125g (4oz) golden caster sugar

3 tbsp crème de cassis

9 thick slices of slightly stale white bread,
crusts removed

1 Put the redcurrants and blackcurrants into a medium pan. Add the sugar and cassis. Bring to a simmer and cook for 3–5 minutes until the sugar has dissolved. Add the raspberries and cook for 2 minutes. Once the fruit is cooked, taste it – there should be a good balance between tart and sweet.

2 Meanwhile, line a 1 litre (1¾ pint) bowl with clingfilm. Put the base of the bowl on one piece of bread and cut around it. Put the circle of bread in the base of the bowl.

3 Line the inside of the bowl with more slices of bread, slightly overlapping to avoid any gaps. Spoon in the fruit, making sure the juice soaks into the bread. Keep back a few spoonfuls of juice in case the bread is unevenly soaked when you turn out the pudding.

4 Cut the remaining bread to fit the top of the pudding neatly, using a sharp knife to trim any excess bread from around the edges. Wrap in clingfilm, weigh down with a saucer and a tin can and chill overnight.

5 To serve, unwrap the outer clingfilm, upturn the pudding on to a plate and remove the inner clingfilm. Drizzle with the reserved juice and serve with crème fraîche or clotted cream.

Serves 8	EASY		NUTRITIONAL INFORMATION	
	Preparation Time 10 minutes, plus overnight chilling	**Cooking Time** 10 minutes	**Per Serving** 173 calories, 1g fat (of which trace saturates), 38g carbohydrate, 0.4g salt	Vegetarian Dairy free

Try Something Different

Use a **cinnamon stick** instead of the star anise.

Nectarines in Spiced Honey and Lemon

4 tbsp clear honey

2 star anise

1 tbsp freshly squeezed lemon juice

150ml (¼ pint) boiling water

4 ripe nectarines or peaches, halved and stoned

vanilla ice cream to serve (optional)

1 Put the honey, star anise and lemon juice into a heatproof bowl. Stir in the boiling water and leave until just warm.

2 Add the nectarines or peaches to the bowl and leave to cool. Transfer to a glass serving dish. Serve with a scoop of vanilla ice cream, if you like.

EASY	NUTRITIONAL INFORMATION		Serves
Preparation Time 10 minutes, plus cooling	**Per Serving** 95 calories, trace fat (of which 0g saturates), 23g carbohydrate, 0g salt	Vegetarian Gluten free • Dairy free	**4**

Try Something Different

Replace the mango with 300ml (½ pint) mixed berry purée and decorate with extra berries,

Mango and Lime Mousse

100ml (3½fl oz) double cream, plus extra to decorate

2 very ripe mangoes, peeled, stoned and sliced

finely grated zest and juice of 2 limes, plus zest of 1 lime to decorate

1 sachet powdered gelatine

3 large eggs, plus 2 yolks

50g (2oz) golden caster sugar

1 Whip the cream until just thick, then chill. Purée the mango flesh in a blender to give 300ml (½ pint).

2 Put 3 tbsp lime juice into a small heatproof bowl, sprinkle the gelatine on top and leave to soak for 10 minutes.

3 In a large bowl, whisk together the eggs, extra yolks and sugar for 4–5 minutes until very thick and mousse-like. Very gently fold in the mango purée, whipped cream and lime zest.

4 Put the gelatine and lime mixture over a pan of boiling water for 1–2 minutes, stir until the gelatine dissolves, then lightly fold into the mango mixture until evenly combined. Divide among six glasses and freeze for 20 minutes, then transfer to the refrigerator to chill for at least 1 hour. To serve, decorate with whipped cream and lime zest.

Serves 6	A LITTLE EFFORT		NUTRITIONAL INFORMATION	
	Preparation Time 25–35 minutes, plus freezing and chilling	**Cooking Time** 1–2 minutes	**Per Serving** 209 calories, 14g fat (of which 7g saturates), 16g carbohydrate, 0.1g salt	Gluten free

Try Something Different

Use raspberries or blueberries instead of the strawberries.

Strawberry Brûlée

250g (9oz) strawberries, hulled and sliced

2 tsp golden icing sugar

1 vanilla pod

400g (14oz) Greek yogurt

100g (3½ oz) golden caster sugar

1 Divide the strawberries among four ramekins and sprinkle with icing sugar.

2 Scrape the seeds from the vanilla pod and stir into the yogurt, then spread the mixture evenly over the fruit.

3 Preheat the grill to high. Sprinkle the caster sugar evenly over the yogurt until it's well covered.

4 Put the ramekins on a baking sheet or into the grill pan and grill until the sugar turns dark brown and caramelises. Leave for 15 minutes or until the caramel is cool enough to eat, or chill for up to 2 hours before serving.

EASY		NUTRITIONAL INFORMATION		Serves
Preparation Time 15 minutes, plus chilling	**Cooking Time** 5 minutes	**Per Serving** 240 calories, 10g fat (of which 5g saturates), 35g carbohydrate, 0.2g salt	Vegetarian • Gluten free	4

Chocolate Mousse Roulade

6 large eggs, separated

150g (5oz) caster sugar, plus extra to sprinkle

50g (2oz) cocoa powder

frosted fruit and leaves to decorate

For the filling

225g (8oz) milk chocolate, roughly chopped

2 large eggs, separated

125g (4oz) fresh or frozen cranberries, halved

50g (2oz) granulated sugar

grated zest and juice of ½ medium orange

200ml (7fl oz) double cream

1 Preheat the oven to 180°C (160°C fan oven) mark 4. Line a 30.5 x 20.5cm (12 x 8in) Swiss roll tin with non-stick baking parchment – it needs to stick up around the edges of the tin by 5cm (2in) to allow the cake to rise.

2 First, make the filling. Put the chocolate into a large heatproof bowl and add 50ml (2fl oz) water. Place over a pan of gently simmering water, making sure the bowl doesn't touch the water. Leave to melt for 15–20 minutes. Remove the bowl from the heat and, without stirring, add the egg yolks, then stir until smooth. In a separate, grease-free bowl, whisk the egg whites until soft peaks form, then fold into the chocolate. Cover and chill for at least 2 hours.

3 Put the cranberries into a pan with the sugar, orange zest and juice and 100ml (3½fl oz) water. Bring to a gentle simmer, then leave to barely simmer for 30 minutes, stirring occasionally until the cranberries are soft; there should be no excess liquid left in the pan. Remove from the heat and leave to cool.

4 To make the cake, put the egg yolks into a bowl and whisk with an electric hand whisk for 1–2 minutes until pale. Add the sugar and whisk until the mixture has the consistency of thick cream. Sift the cocoa powder over the mixture and fold in with a large metal spoon. In a separate, grease-free bowl, whisk the egg whites until soft peaks form. Stir a spoonful of the egg whites into the chocolate mixture to loosen it, then fold in the remainder. Pour the mixture into the prepared tin and bake for about 25 minutes or until well risen and spongy. Leave to cool completely in the tin (it will sink dramatically).

5 When cold, put a sheet of baking parchment on the worksurface and sprinkle with caster sugar. Turn the cake out on to the sugar and peel off the parchment. Spoon the chocolate filling on top and spread to within 2.5cm (1in) of the edge. Sprinkle on the glazed cranberries. Lightly whip the cream, spoon over the cranberries, then spread lightly to cover.

6 Holding a short edge of the baking parchment, gently lift and roll, pushing the edge down so it starts to curl. Keep lifting and rolling as the cake comes away from the paper. Don't worry if it cracks. Remove the paper. Chill for up to 8 hours. Decorate with frosted fruit and leaves.

Serves 8	FOR THE CONFIDENT COOK		NUTRITIONAL INFORMATION	
	Preparation Time 45 minutes, plus 2 hours chilling	**Cooking Time** 40 minutes, plus cooling	**Per Serving** 510 calories, 30g fat (of which 16g saturates), 53g carbohydrate, 0.4g salt	Vegetarian • Gluten free

Cook's Tip

Sweet Shortcrust Pastry: sift 175g (6oz) plain flour with a pinch of salt into a bowl and add 75g (3oz) unsalted butter, cut into small pieces. Using your fingertips, rub the butter into the flour until the mixture resembles fine breadcrumbs. Using a fork, mix in 3 large egg yolks, 75g (3oz) caster sugar and 1½ tsp water until the mixture holds together; add a little more water if necessary. Knead lightly. Form into a ball, wrap tightly in clingfilm and chill for at least 30 minutes before using. (This 'relaxes' the pastry and prevents shrinkage when it is baked.)

Glazed Brandied Prune Tart

1 quantity Sweet Shortcrust Pastry (see Cook's Tip)
flour to dust

For the filling
250g (9oz) ready-to-eat pitted prunes
5 tbsp brandy
1 vanilla pod, split
150ml (¼ pint) double cream
150ml (¼ pint) single cream
25g (1oz) caster sugar
2 large eggs
4 tbsp apricot jam and 2 tbsp brandy to glaze

1 To make the filling, put the prunes into a small bowl, add the brandy, then cover and leave to soak overnight or for several hours.

2 Roll out the pastry on a lightly floured surface and use to line a 23cm (9in), 2.5cm (1in) deep, loose-based fluted flan tin. Chill for 30 minutes. Preheat the oven to 200°C (180°C fan oven) mark 6. Prick the pastry base with a fork, then bake blind (see page 116). Reduce the oven temperature to 180°C (160°C fan oven) mark 4.

3 Put the vanilla pod into a pan with the double cream. Bring just to the boil. Remove from the heat and leave to infuse for 20 minutes. Remove the vanilla pod, rinse, dry and store for reuse. Pour the cream into a bowl. Add the single cream, sugar and eggs and beat well.

4 Scatter the prunes over the pastry case, then pour the cream mixture around them. Bake for 30 minutes or until the custard is turning golden and is just set in the centre.

5 Meanwhile, sieve the jam into a pan, add the brandy and heat gently until smooth. Brush the glaze over the tart and serve warm or cold.

Serves 8	EASY		NUTRITIONAL INFORMATION	
	Preparation Time 25 minutes, plus overnight soaking, plus chilling	**Cooking Time** 50 minutes	**Per Serving** 440 calories, 24g fat (of which 14g saturates), 47g carbohydrate, 0.2g salt	Vegetarian

Get Ahead

Complete the recipe, cover and chill for up to two days.

125g (4oz) golden caster sugar

pared zest of 1 orange

5 sheets leaf gelatine

75cl bottle champagne or sparkling wine

2–3 tbsp orange-flavoured liqueur,
such as Grand Marnier

edible gold leaf to decorate

Champagne Jellies

1 Put the sugar into a pan. Add the orange zest and 250ml (9fl oz) cold water and heat gently until the sugar dissolves. Bring the mixture to the boil, then simmer gently for 2–3 minutes until slightly reduced and syrupy. Remove the pan from the heat and discard the orange zest.

2 Meanwhile, put the gelatine into a shallow bowl and cover with cold water. Leave to soak for 5 minutes.

3 Lift the gelatine out of the bowl, squeeze out the excess water, then add it to the pan. Stir gently for 2–3 minutes until the gelatine dissolves completely.

4 Pour the champagne and liqueur into the pan, then transfer the mixture to a jug. Fill eight wine glasses with the jelly mixture, then chill for 4 hours or until set. Decorate with gold leaf to serve.

EASY		NUTRITIONAL INFORMATION		Serves
Preparation Time 15 minutes, plus chilling	**Cooking Time** 15 minutes	**Per Serving** 165 calories, trace fat (of which 0g saturates), 21g carbohydrate, 0g salt	Gluten free • Dairy free	**8**

Pear and Ginger Steamed Pudding

125g (4oz) butter, softened, plus extra for greasing

1 large pear, peeled, cored and diced

2 tbsp golden caster sugar

2 balls stem ginger, finely chopped, plus 2 tbsp ginger syrup

4 tbsp golden syrup

125g (4oz) light muscovado sugar

finely grated zest of 1 lemon

2 medium eggs, beaten

175g (6oz) self-raising flour

2 tsp ground ginger

3 tbsp perry or pear juice

1 Grease a 900ml (1½ pint) pudding basin. Put the pear into a pan with 2 tbsp water and the caster sugar and simmer for 5 minutes. Stir in the stem ginger and the ginger and golden syrups and leave to cool. Tip into the basin.

2 Beat the butter, muscovado sugar and lemon zest in a bowl with an electric hand whisk until light and fluffy. Beat in the eggs a little at a time.

3 Fold in the flour and ground ginger, then fold in the perry or pear juice. Pour the mixture into the basin on top of the pear compote. Cut out a piece each of greaseproof and tin foil, each measuring 30.5 x 30.5cm (12 x 12in). Fold a pleat in the middle; put on top of pudding. Tie under rim with string, using extra to make a knotted handle over the top. Trim excess paper and foil.

4 Sit the basin on an upturned saucer in a large pan. Pour in enough boiling water to come halfway up the basin. Cover and steam for 1¼–1½ hours, topping up with extra boiling water when necessary. Turn out on to a plate and serve.

EASY			NUTRITIONAL INFORMATION		Serves
Preparation Time 20 minutes	Cooking Time 1 hour 35 minutes		Per Serving 314 calories, 14g fat (of which 9g saturates), 45g carbohydrate, 0.6g salt	Vegetarian	8

White Chocolate Mousse Cake

vegetable oil to grease
450g (1lb) white chocolate, roughly chopped
300ml (½ pint) double cream
finely grated zest of 1 large orange
2 tsp orange liqueur, such as Grand Marnier
300g (11oz) full-fat Greek yogurt
halved strawberries, a handful of blueberries and a handful of unsprayed rose petals to decorate
icing sugar to dust

1 Lightly oil a shallow 20cm (8in) round cake tin and line with baking parchment.

2 Put the chocolate into a large bowl with half the cream. Bring a large pan of water to the boil, remove from the heat and sit the bowl of chocolate and cream on top, making sure the base of the bowl doesn't touch the water. Leave for 20–30 minutes until the chocolate has melted. Don't stir; just leave it to melt.

3 Meanwhile, put the orange zest and liqueur into a small bowl and set aside to soak. Whip the remaining cream until it just holds its shape.

4 Remove the bowl of melted chocolate from the pan and beat in the yogurt. Fold in the cream with the zest and liqueur mixture. Spoon the mixture into the prepared tin, cover with clingfilm and freeze overnight or for up to one month.

5 One hour before serving, transfer from the freezer to the refrigerator. Unwrap and put on a serving plate. Decorate with fruit and petals and dust lightly with icing sugar.

Serves	EASY		NUTRITIONAL INFORMATION	
10	**Preparation Time** 30 minutes, plus overnight freezing	**Cooking Time** 20–30 minutes	**Per Serving** 416 calories, 32g fat (of which 19g saturates), 27g carbohydrate, 0.2g salt	Vegetarian • Gluten free

150ml (¼ pint) port

150ml (¼ pint) freshly squeezed orange juice

75g (3oz) light muscovado sugar

1 cinnamon stick

6 cardamom pods, lightly crushed

5cm (2in) piece fresh root ginger, peeled and thinly sliced

50g (2oz) large muscatel raisins or dried blueberries

1 small pineapple, peeled, cored and thinly sliced

1 mango, peeled, stoned and thickly sliced

3 tangerines, peeled and halved horizontally

3 fresh figs, halved

Spiced Winter Fruit

1 First, make the syrup. Pour the port and orange juice into a small pan, then add the sugar and 300ml (½ pint) cold water. Bring to the boil, stirring all the time. Add the cinnamon stick, cardamom pods and ginger, then bubble gently for 15 minutes.

2 Put all the fruit into a serving bowl. Remove the cinnamon stick and cardamom pods from the syrup – or leave in for a spicier flavour – then pour the syrup over the fruit. Serve warm or cold.

EASY		NUTRITIONAL INFORMATION		Serves
Preparation Time 20 minutes, plus cooling	**Cooking Time** 20 minutes	**Per Serving** 207 calories, trace fat (of which 0g saturates), 45g carbohydrate, 0g salt	Vegetarian Gluten free • Dairy free	**6**

Cook's Tip

To bake blind, prick the pastry base with a fork. Cover with foil or greaseproof paper 7.5cm (3in) larger than the tin and spread baking beans on top. Bake for 15–20 minutes. Remove the foil or paper and beans and bake for 5–10 minutes until the pastry is light golden.

Coconut and Mango Tart

125g (4oz) plain flour, plus extra to dust

75g (3oz) firm unsalted butter

1 tbsp caster sugar

40g (1½oz) desiccated coconut

1 medium egg yolk

toasted coconut shreds to decorate

icing sugar to dust

For the filling

2 small ripe mangoes, peeled, stoned and thinly sliced

75ml (2½fl oz) freshly squeezed orange juice

2 tbsp caster sugar, plus 75g (3oz)

3 medium eggs

15g (½oz) cornflour

400ml can coconut milk

150ml (¼ pint) double cream

1 To make the pastry, whiz the flour and butter in a food processor until the mixture resembles fine crumbs. Stir in the caster sugar and coconut. Add the egg yolk and about 2 tbsp cold water and pulse to make a firm dough. Knead lightly, wrap and chill for 30 minutes. Preheat the oven to 200°C (180°C fan oven) mark 6. Roll out the pastry on a lightly floured surface and use to line a 23cm (9in), 4cm (1½in) deep, loose-based flan tin. Bake blind (see Cook's Tip). Reduce the oven temperature to 150°C (130°C fan oven) mark 2.

2 Meanwhile, to make the filling, put the mango slices in a heavy-based pan with the orange juice and 2 tbsp caster sugar. Bring to a simmer and cook gently for 3–5 minutes until the mango slices are softened but still retain their shape. Cool slightly.

3 Beat the eggs and the remaining sugar together in a bowl. Blend the cornflour with a little of the coconut milk in a pan. Add the remaining coconut milk and bring to the boil, stirring until thickened. Remove from the heat and stir in the cream. Pour over the egg mixture, stirring until smooth.

4 Drain the mangoes, reserving the juice, and arrange in the pastry case. Stir the reserved juice into the coconut custard and ladle it over the mangoes. Bake for about 30 minutes until the custard is just set; it will continue to firm up as it cools. Leave to cool, then chill for several hours or overnight. Decorate with coconut shreds and dust with icing sugar.

Serves 6	EASY		NUTRITIONAL INFORMATION	
	Preparation Time 35 minutes, plus 3–4 hours chilling	**Cooking Time** 50 minutes, plus cooling	**Per Serving** 253 calories, 18g fat (of which 11g saturates), 20g carbohydrate, 0.3g salt	Vegetarian

Cook's Tip

Poached Rhubarb: chop 250g (9oz) rhubarb into 6.5cm (2½in) pieces. Put into a pan with 50g (2oz) caster sugar, 25g (1oz) stem ginger, cut into slivers, and 75ml (3fl oz) water. Cover and simmer gently for 5 minutes.

Get Ahead

Complete the recipe without icing sugar up to one day in advance. Store in an airtight container.
To use Dust with icing sugar to serve.

Rhubarb Crumble Cake

150g (5oz) unsalted butter, softened, plus extra to grease
400g (14oz) rhubarb, trimmed and cut into 2.5cm (1in) pieces
175g (6oz) golden caster sugar
2 large eggs, beaten
100g (3½oz) ground almonds
3 tbsp milk
125g (4oz) self-raising flour
1 tsp cinnamon
½ tsp ground ginger
50g (2oz) flaked almonds
icing sugar to dust
Poached Rhubarb to serve (see Cook's Tip)

For the crumble topping
40g (1½oz) cold unsalted butter, diced
50g (2oz) plain flour
40g (1½oz) demerara sugar

1 Grease and line a 20.5cm (8in) springform tin. Put the rhubarb into a pan with 25g (1oz) caster sugar and 100ml (3½fl oz) water and simmer for 5 minutes. Strain and set aside.

2 To make the topping, rub the chilled diced butter into the flour until the mixture resembles breadcrumbs. Stir in the demerara sugar and set aside.

3 Preheat the oven to 180°C (160°C fan oven) mark 4. Beat the softened butter and remaining caster sugar until pale and fluffy. Gradually add the eggs, beating well after each addition. Using a large metal spoon, fold in the ground almonds, milk, flour and spices, then fold in the flaked almonds. Turn into the prepared tin, level the surface and top with rhubarb, then sprinkle with crumble topping. Bake for 1–1¼ hours until a skewer inserted in the centre comes out clean. Leave for 5 minutes before removing from the tin. Dust with icing sugar and serve warm with custard and poached rhubarb, or cool on a wire rack and serve cold.

Serves 10	EASY		NUTRITIONAL INFORMATION	
	Preparation Time 25 minutes	**Cooking Time** 1 hour–1 hour 20 minutes	**Per Serving** 394 calories, 25g fat (of which 11g saturates), 37g carbohydrate, 0.5g salt	Vegetarian

Italian Ice Cream Cake

400g (14oz) fresh cherries, pitted and quartered

4 tbsp Amaretto

10 tbsp crème de cacao (chocolate liqueur)

200g (7oz) Savoiardi biscuits or sponge fingers

5 medium egg yolks

150g (5oz) golden caster sugar

450ml (¾ pint) double cream, lightly whipped

1 tbsp vanilla extract

75g (3oz) pistachio nuts or hazelnuts, roughly chopped

75g (3oz) plain chocolate, roughly chopped

2–3 tbsp cocoa powder

2–3 tbsp golden icing sugar

1 Put the cherries and Amaretto into a bowl, stir, cover and put to one side. Pour the crème de cacao into a shallow dish. Quickly dip a sponge finger into the liqueur – on one side only, so that it doesn't go soggy and fall apart – then put on to a large chopping board and cut in half lengthways to separate the sugary side from the base. Repeat with each biscuit.

2 Double line a 23cm (9in) round, 4cm (1½in) deep tin with clingfilm. Arrange the sugar-coated sponge finger halves, sugar side down, on the base of the tin. Drizzle with any remaining crème de cacao.

3 Put the egg yolks and caster sugar into a large bowl and whisk until pale and fluffy. Fold in the cream, vanilla extract, nuts, chocolate and cherries, plus any remaining Amaretto. Spoon over the sponge fingers in the tin and cover with the remaining sponge finger halves, cut side down. Cover with clingfilm and freeze for at least 5 hours.

4 To serve, upturn the cake on to a serving plate and remove the clingfilm. Sift cocoa and icing sugar over the cake and leave at room temperature for 20 minutes if the weather is warm, 40 minutes at cool room temperature, or 1 hour in the refrigerator, to allow the cherries to thaw and the ice cream to become moussey. Slice and serve.

EASY	NUTRITIONAL INFORMATION		Serves
Preparation Time 40 minutes, plus 5 hours freezing	**Per Serving** 522 calories, 33g fat (of which 15g saturates), 46g carbohydrate, 0.2g salt	Vegetarian	**4**

White Chocolate and Raspberry Tart

150g (5oz) plain flour
pinch of salt
65g (2¹/₂oz) cold, unsalted butter, diced
100g (3¹/₂oz) ground hazelnuts
25g (1oz) sugar
1 large egg, beaten
250g tub mascarpone
200g (7oz) bar good-quality white chocolate
142ml carton double cream
400g (14oz) fresh raspberries
golden icing sugar to dust

1   Sift the flour and salt into a food processor. Add the butter and whiz until the mixture resembles fine breadcrumbs. Add the hazelnuts, sugar and just enough egg to bring the mixture together – use the pulse button to help you. Shape the pastry into a disc, wrap in clingfilm and chill for 30 minutes.

2   Roll out the pastry, then press into the base and sides of a 20.5cm (8in) fluted pastry tin. Prick all over. Cover with a large circle of baking parchment and top with baking beans. Chill until firm. Preheat the oven to 190°C (170°C fan oven) mark 5.

3   Bake for 12–15 minutes until the pastry has set. Remove the beans and parchment and continue baking for 5–10 minutes until the pastry is dry and slightly sandy to the touch. Cool in the tin on a wire rack.

4   Melt the mascarpone and chocolate together in a heatproof bowl set over a pan of gently simmering water, making sure the base of the bowl doesn't touch the water. Don't stir, otherwise the mixture will thicken into a sticky mess.

5   Remove the bowl from the pan and set aside to cool completely. Meanwhile, lightly whip the cream. Fold the chocolate into the cream. Spoon the filling into the pastry case and chill. To serve, top with raspberries and dust with icing sugar.

EASY		NUTRITIONAL INFORMATION		Serves
Preparation Time 35 minutes, plus chilling	**Cooking Time** 30 minutes	**Per Serving** 391 calories, 32g fat (of which 16g saturates), 24g carbohydrate, 0.3g salt	Vegetarian	**12**

Cook's Tip

Freeze the leftover egg whites in a clean container for up to three months and use to make meringues.

Custard Tart

225g (8oz) plain flour, sifted, plus extra to dust
175g (6oz) cold butter, diced
50g (2oz) golden caster sugar
finely grated zest of 1 lemon
1 medium egg yolk

For the filling

8 large egg yolks
75g (3oz) golden caster sugar
450ml (³/₄ pint) single cream
nutmeg for grating

1 Put the flour into a bowl and rub in the butter until it resembles breadcrumbs. Stir in the sugar and zest. Lightly beat the egg yolk with 2–3 tbsp ice-cold water and, using a knife, stir small amounts into the flour until it starts to clump together but isn't too sticky or dry. Bring together with your hands. Knead lightly until smooth. Shape into a disc, wrap in clingfilm and chill for 30 minutes.

2 Roll out the pastry on a lightly floured surface to a 3mm (¹/₈in) thickness. Use to line a 23cm (9in) round, 4cm (1¹/₂in) deep flan tin. Prick the base and chill for 30 minutes. Preheat the oven to 200°C (180°C fan oven) mark 6 and put the tin on to a baking sheet. Line the tin with greaseproof paper, cover with baking beans and bake for 12–15 minutes. Remove the beans and paper and continue baking for 5–10 minutes until cooked through. Reduce the oven temperature to 130°C (110°C fan oven) mark ¹/₂.

3 Mix the egg yolks and sugar together with a wooden spoon. Gradually stir in the cream, then strain into a jug to remove any eggy strands. Pour the mixture into the pastry case and bake for 40–50 minutes until just set with a little wobble. Grate over plenty of nutmeg and cool in the tin on a wire rack. Serve at room temperature.

Serves 10	EASY		NUTRITIONAL INFORMATION	
	Preparation Time 25 minutes, plus chilling	**Cooking Time** 1¹/₄ hours	**Per Serving** 399 calories, 28g fat (of which 16g saturates), 32g carbohydrate, 0.4g salt	Vegetarian

Get Ahead

Complete the recipe, without icing sugar, up to two days in advance or freeze for up to one month. Keep in the dish, wrapped in clingfilm.
To use If frozen, thaw at cool room temperature overnight; remove 1 hour before serving. Dust with icing sugar and serve.

Marbled Chocolate Cheesecake

150g (5oz) digestive biscuits, crushed

100g (3¹/₂oz) ground almonds

75g (3oz) unsalted butter, melted

75g (3oz) plain chocolate

5 large eggs, separated

150g (5oz) golden caster sugar

600g (1lb 5oz) full-fat cream cheese

1¹/₂ tsp vanilla bean paste

golden icing sugar to dust (optional)

1 Line a 33 x 23 x 5cm (13 x 9 x 2in) roasting tin with greaseproof paper, leaving the excess hanging over the sides. Mix together the biscuits, almonds and butter and press into the base. Chill.

2 Preheat the oven to 170°C (150°C fan oven) mark 3. Melt the chocolate in a heatproof bowl set over a pan of just simmering water (the bowl shouldn't touch the water). Don't stir, or it will congeal. Cool slightly.

3 Whisk the egg whites until soft peaks form. Add 25g (1oz) sugar and whisk until stiff peaks form. In a separate bowl, using the same whisk, mix the cream cheese, remaining sugar, yolks and vanilla. Using a metal spoon, stir a spoonful of egg white into the cheese mixture. Carefully fold in the remaining whites. Put a quarter of the mixture into the egg white bowl. Fold the chocolate into it. Pour the vanilla mixture over the biscuit base, dollop spoonfuls of chocolate mixture on top and marble using a knife. Bake for 45 minutes or until set. Cool in the tin. Chill for 2 hours. Remove from the tin and dust with icing sugar, if you like.

EASY		NUTRITIONAL INFORMATION		Serves
Preparation Time 25 minutes, plus chilling	**Cooking Time** 45 minutes	**Per Serving** 325 calories, 27g fat (of which 14g saturates), 18g carbohydrate, 0.5g salt	Vegetarian	**18**

Freezing Tip

To freeze Complete the recipe to the end of step 6. Wrap the cake in clingfilm and put the syrup into a sealed freezerproof box. Label and freeze for up to three months.

To use Thaw the cake and syrup at cool room temperature the day before; make the ganache, cover and chill. On the day, complete the recipe; cover the cake loosely and chill until needed.

Orange and White Chocolate Cake

6 large eggs, separated
250g (9oz) golden caster sugar
150g (5oz) each self-raising flour and ground almonds
grated zest of 2 oranges

For the syrup
100g (3½oz) golden granulated sugar
225ml (8fl oz) sweet white wine
juice of 3 large oranges

For the white chocolate ganache
225g (8oz) white chocolate, chopped
568ml carton double cream
350g (12oz) strawberries, thinly sliced

1 Grease a deep 23cm (9in) round cake tin. Line the base with greaseproof paper. Preheat the oven to 180°C (160°C fan oven) mark 4.

2 Put the egg whites into a bowl and whisk until soft peaks form. Gradually beat in 50g (2oz) sugar. Whisk until the mixture stands in stiff peaks and looks glossy. Put the egg yolks and remaining sugar into another bowl. Whisk until soft and moussey. Carefully stir in the flour to make a paste. Using a clean metal spoon, add a third of the egg white to the paste and fold in carefully. Put the remaining egg white, ground almonds and orange zest into the bowl and gently fold in. You should end up with a smooth batter. Spoon into the tin and bake for 35 minutes or until a skewer run through the centre comes out clean. Cool in the tin for 10 minutes, then turn out on to a wire rack to cool completely.

3 Put the syrup ingredients into a small pan and stir over a gentle heat until the sugar has dissolved. Bring to the boil and bubble for 5 minutes or until syrupy. Cool and set aside.

4 To make the ganache, put the chocolate into a heatproof bowl with half the cream. Set over a pan of simmering water, making sure the bowl doesn't touch the water, leave until the chocolate is melted, then stir. (Don't stir before.) Cool until beginning to thicken, then beat with a wooden spoon until cold and thick. Put the remaining double cream into a bowl and whip lightly. Beat a large spoonful into the chocolate cream to loosen it, then fold in the remainder. Cover and chill for 2 hours.

5 Cut the cake in half horizontally, pierce all over with a skewer and put it, cut sides up, on an edged tray. Spoon the syrup over and leave to soak in. Spread a quarter of the ganache over the base cake. Scatter with 225g (8oz) strawberries. Cover with the top half of the cake and press down lightly. Using a palette knife, smooth the remaining ganache over the top and sides of the cake. Cover loosely and chill for up to 4 hours. Decorate with the remaining strawberries.

Serves	EASY		NUTRITIONAL INFORMATION	
14	**Preparation Time** 35 minutes	**Cooking Time** 35–40 minutes, plus 2 hours chilling	**Per Serving** 525 calories, 35g fat (of which 16g saturates), 49g carbohydrate, 0.2g salt	Vegetarian

Cook's Tip

If you're using an ice-cream maker, add the whisked egg white halfway through churning, which will give the sorbet a creamier texture.

Orange Sorbet

grated zest of 3 oranges and juice of 6 oranges – you'll need around 600ml (1 pint)

200g (7oz) golden granulated sugar

1 tbsp orange flower water

1 medium egg white

Medjool dates, sliced, and 1 orange, cut into segments, to decorate

1 Pour 300ml (½ pint) water into a large pan, add the orange zest and sugar and bring slowly to the boil. Stir occasionally with a wooden spoon to dissolve the sugar and simmer for 5 minutes. Leave to cool for 1–2 minutes, then strain the syrup into a clean bowl.

2 Strain the orange juice into the cooled syrup and stir in the orange flower water. Chill for 30 minutes.

3 Pour the mixture into a shallow 18cm (7in) square freezerproof container and freeze for 3 hours until slushy. Whisk the egg white until stiff, then fold into the mixture. Put the sorbet back in the freezer and freeze until solid – about 2 hours or overnight.

4 Put the sorbet in the refrigerator for 15–20 minutes before serving to soften slightly. Decorate with Medjool dates and orange segments.

Serves	EASY		NUTRITIONAL INFORMATION	
6	**Preparation Time** 20 minutes, plus chilling and 5 hours freezing	**Cooking Time** 10 minutes	**Per Serving** 169 calories, trace fat, 44g carbohydrate, 0.1g salt	Vegetarian Dairy free • Gluten free

Index